Adobe Angels-T

In this book, Antonio Garcez has succeeded in introducing the reader to a world where the supernatural is alive. The book explores the hopes and fears of this world with the startling imagery of the next. I highly recommend that both local citizens and visitors to Santa Fe read ADOBE ANGELS-THE GHOSTS OF SANTA FE.
Sam Pick, Mayor-Santa Fe, New Mexico

This collection of personal encounters with the 'spiritual' or 'supernatural' certainly supported some of my own experiences.
Stephanie Gonzales, NM Secretary of State

A faceless man, a ghostly nun, and New Mexico's most famous spirit, La llorona, who weeps forever for her lost children. Based on interviews with people who experienced these ghosts, there are some real chillers here, particularly the stories of witchcraft. Garcez says this is the first in a series of books on the ghosts of New Mexico. I know I'm looking forward to the next one!
Chris Woodyard, *Invisible Ink*-Books on Ghosts & Hauntings

We can't get enough of this genre and, mercy knows, we have plenty of ghosts tales for many books to come. These however are not second-hand tales, but stories from people who have witnessed and experienced the strange and ghostly in the City Different.
Dwight A. Myers, Exec. Dir., New Mexico Book League

The past often intrudes upon the present, influencing it in many ways. In this work Garcez, after much interviewing and research, gives voice to some of those powerful, restless spirits of the past who continue to frequent Santa Fe. The tales (and the ghosts) range from the innocuous to the eerie.
TST, Books Of The Southwest

At last someone has written a book about the ghost tales people have been telling here for years!
Tom Sharpe, Albuquerque Journal

It's enough to send shivers right up your spine! An excellent first effort by Antonio Garcez and I anxiously await his next book!
Dale Kaczmarek, Ghost Research Society

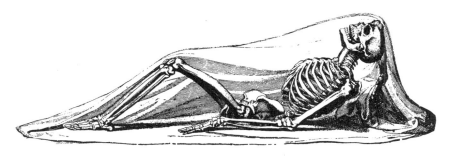

© Copyright 1995 by Antonio R. Garcez
All Rights Reserved

To inquire about scheduling the author for public appearances,
you may write to the address below.

Antonio R. Garcez
c/o Red Rabbit Press
P.O. Box 6545
Santa Fe, NM 87502-6545

No part of this book may be reproduced in any form or by any electronic or mechanical means including information storage and retrieval systems, without permission in writing from the publisher, except by a reviewer who may quote brief passages in a review.

All photos were taken by the author, except where otherwise noted.

Revised Edition

Printed in the United States of America

Library of Congress Catalog Card Number: 95-070303
ISBN Number 0-9634029-3-5

Published in 1995 by
Red Rabbit Press
P.O. Box 6545
Santa Fe, New Mexico 87502-6545

Acknowledgments

I wish to thank the following individuals for their support and assistance:

Hank Estrada
Juanita C. Vigil
Rev. John Ludwig
Stephanie Gonzales, New Mexico Secretary of State
Sam Pick, Former Santa Fe City Mayor
Frederick A. Peralta, Town of Taos Mayor
Skip Keith Miller, Hacienda Martinez History
Taos Art Association, Stables Art Center History
Taos Chamber of Commerce, City of Taos and Taos Pueblo History

and especially to every person whom
I interviewed for this book.

Dedication

To my ancestors.

And to my partner, Hank Estrada,
who dreams with me.

I personally want to extend my gratitude to all the excellent teachers in New Mexico who tirelessly and daily attempt to make positive changes in their students lives.

Society will always be in trouble as long as we pay the best teachers less than the worst football coach.

Table of Contents

History of the Flag of the State of New Mexico 1
History of the Great Seal of the State of New Mexico 2
Foreword
    Stephanie Gonzales, NM Secretary of State 4
    Sam Pick, Former Santa Fe Mayor 5
    Frederick A. Peralta, Town of Taos Mayor 6
Preface 7
Introduction 14

SANTA FE
Sister George
    History 17
    Early Apparitions 18
    Recent Happenings 19
    June Key's Story 20
    Melinda's Story 22
    Chronology 25
Grant Corner Inn 26
    Art Garcia's Story 29
Doña Leticia
    Alberto Sena's Story 38
The House on Apodaca Hill 42
    Patricia's Story 43
    Jonathan's Story 50
Guadalupe & La Llorona
    Guadalupe's Story 52
Canyon Road
    William Auclair's Story 55
The Legal Tender 58
    Emma Cordova's Story 59
    Raymond Taylor's Stories 62
Casa Real
    David Rodriguez's Story 65
    The Lady in Room 222 69
La Posada Hotel 71
Florencita's Story 76

El Zorrillo's Story 78
Ten Thousand Waves 85
   Duke's Story 86
St. Vincent Hospital
   Maryclare's Story 90
La Residencia 94
   The Nurse Coordinator's Story: Blood in the Basement . . . 95
   Room 311 98
   The Nurse Assistant's Story: The Call Light 101
   The Charge Nurse Story: Room 311 103
   Footsteps in the Hall 105
Poor Michael
   Evelina's Story 108
Sofita Becera 115
   El Molcajete 117

TAOS

Historic Taos 122
History of the Mabel Dodge Luhan House 125
   Maria E. Fortin's Story 126
The Garden Restaurant
   Larry C. Tibbetts Story 130
   Anna M. Johnson's Story 132
   Earl P. White's Story 134
The Hacienda Martinez
   History 136
   Restoration 137
   Elma Torres' Story 139
   Dolores I. Struck's Story 143
The Stables Art Center 145
   Arthur R. Manby House Chronology 147
   Vikki E. Madden's Story 148
"Gramps"
   Bobbie A. Gonzales' Story 151
Windsong Gallery
   Wendy Wysong's Story 155
Taos Pueblo 159
   Alfred J. Montoya's Story 161

History of the Flag of the State of New Mexico

The first flag of New Mexico statehood was designed by New Mexico historian Ralph Emerson Twitchell as authorized in 1915. It consisted of a blue field with a miniature United States flag in the upper left corner, the state's great seal in the lower right corner, and "New Mexico" embroidered diagonally across the field from the lower left to the upper right corner.

In 1920, the New Mexico Chapter of the Daughters of the American Revolution (D.A.R.) advocated the adoption of a flag representative of New Mexico's unique character. Three years later, the D.A.R. conducted a design competition which was won by the distinguished Santa Fe physician and archeologist, Dr. Harry Mera. The doctor's wife Reba, made the winning flag design with a symbolic red zia on a field of gold. In March of 1925, Governor Arthur T. Hannett signed the legislation which proclaimed the Mera design as the official state flag.

The State Flag of New Mexico has a modern interpretation of an ancient symbol of a sun design as seen on a late 19th century water jar from Zia Pueblo. This pueblo is thought to have been one of the Seven Golden Cities of Cibola, which explorer Vasques de Coronado sought. The red sun symbol was then call a "Zia" and is shown on a field of gold. Red and gold are the colors of Queen Isabella of Castille which the Spanish Conquistadores brought to the New World.

The flags of Spain, the Republic of Mexico, the Confederate States of America, and the United States of America have all flown over the "Land of Enchantment" during the long history of the state.

Official Salute to the Flag

English-*"I salute the flag of the State of New Mexico and the Zia symbol of perfect friendship among united cultures."*

The words of the salute were composed by the Ellen Jones Chapter of the United Daughters of the Confederacy under the authority of Mrs. W. B. Oldham, and the state salute was adopted by the 26th Legislature on March 13, 1963.

Spanish-*"Saludo la bandera del estado de Nuevo Mejico, el simbolo Zia de amistad perfecta, entre culturas unidas."* Translated by Maria E. Naranjo of Larragoite School in Santa Fe, and adopted by the 31st Legislature in 1973.

History of the Great Seal of the State of New Mexico

The first Great Seal was designed shortly after the organization of the Territory of New Mexico in 1851. The original has long since disappeared. According to early imprints, it consisted of the American Bald Eagle, as portrayed on the Great Seal of the United States, shielding the smaller Mexican Eagle within its outstretched wings, thus symbolizing the change of sovereignty from Mexico to the United States in 1846.

The American Bald Eagle, which has always represented bravery, skill and strength, clasped three arrows in its talons. The smaller, Mexican Brown (or Harpy) Eagle, grasped a snake in its beak and cactus in its talons. This portion of the seal is still the official symbol of the Mexican Republic and portrays the ancient Aztec myth which says the gods ordered the Aztec Indians to settle the site in which they saw an eagle poised upon a cactus devouring a serpent. The scroll below the eagles contained the phrase, *Crescit Eundo*, which translated from the Latin is, "It grows as it goes."

In 1882, Territorial Secretary W.G. Ritch, embellished the original design with the addition of background figures depicting industry and agriculture and used his design for territorial documents. In 1887, the original seal was officially adopted by act of the Territorial Legislature with the addition of the 1850 date at the bottom.

When New Mexico became a state in 1912, the second session of the First Legislature named a commission for the purpose of adopting a state seal. After the commission had filed a certificate of its choice of design with the Secretary of State, that official was authorized to procure a seal in accordance with the certificate. Until such time as the new seal was accepted, the Secretary of State was directed to use the territorial seal with the word, STATE substituted for the word, TERRITORY. The certificate of the commission's choice does not appear to have been actually filed however, but its decision must have been to continue to use the territorial seal with the changing of territory to state and with the substitution of the 1912 date of statehood for the 1850 at the bottom of the seal.

Stephanie Gonzales
Secretary of State—1991-1995

STEPHANIE GONZALES	STATE of NEW MEXICO
Secretary of State	Santa Fe

OFFICE of the SECRETARY of STATE

Dear Fellow Readers,

New Mexico, and especially Santa Fe, has long been known as a place like no other on earth. This author has captured in the contents of his book one of the reasons why it is so unique. It is a spiritual haven and has always been so, thanks to the deep and serious faith embedded in our people's cultures and traditions.

This collection of personal encounters with the "spiritual" or "supernatural" certainly supported some of my own experiences and caused me to again reflect and appreciate those very special moments.

Mr. Garcez, a local sympatico, has been able to obtain those personal memories that are rarely shared, particularly by some of our more guarded but beloved elders. We are most fortunate that such a sensitive person was able to create a safe place and opportunity for the recording of these exceptional experiences. He is to be commended for accomplishing this documentation and presenting it in a most believable manner. I recommend you turn the page and travel on "the path" that will help you with your "knowing."

Sincerely,

Stephanie Gonzales

STEPHANIE GONZALES
Secretary of State
State of New Mexico

City of Santa Fe, New Mexico

P.O. BOX 909, 200 LINCOLN AVE., 87504-0909
(505) 984-6590

SAM PICK, *Mayor*

Adobe Angels—The Ghosts of Santa Fe

In this book, Antonio Garcez has succeeded in introducing the reader to a world where the supernatural is alive. The book explores the hopes and fears of this world with the startling imagery of the next. I highly recommend that both local citizens and visitors to Santa Fe read *Adobe Angels*.

Sam Pick

SAM PICK
Mayor
City of Santa Fe

OFFICE of the MAYOR

Taos Municipal Building, 400 Camino de la Placita (505) 751-2006 FAX 751-2026
Taos, New Mexico 87571

FREDERICK A. PERALTA, MAYOR

Adobe Angels—The Ghosts of Santa Fe and Taos

Readers familiar with Antonio R. Garcez's superb first book, *Adobe Angels—The Ghosts of Santa Fe* will not be disappointed with his second revised edition, *Adobe Angels—The Ghosts of Santa Fe and Taos*. Mr. Garcez's ability to research and seek out those particular individuals who have had first hand encounters with the supernatural is admirable. Most importantly is the way Mr. Garcez sets you up by providing you with the history behind the story.

Fascinating to read, *Adobe Angels—The Ghosts of Santa Fe and Taos* offers the reader insight into our town's unique traditions, folklore and history; don't miss it!

FREDERICK A. PERALTA
Mayor
Town of Taos

Preface

In beginning the research for this first collection of stories about the ghosts of Santa Fe and Taos, I embarked on a journey through my own life, taking a path I had always been aware of but had not traveled for many years. I was forced to reflect on the memories of my childhood and the strong ties of spirituality: the Catholic religion, Native American healing, and the cultural traditions of my parents, who remained cautious of the larger society in which they lived. Why not a book on . . . say, woodpeckers, wallpaper or tangerines? Instead, I subconsciously chose a subject which was as much a part of me as the stride of my walk or the part in my hair, for I understood that the indefinite confines of spirits, ghosts, angels, and guardians were everpresent and vital to us, the living. Their presence in our world represent a warehouse of direction, intervention, power and introspective knowledge for us to tap into.

During the many interviews for this book, I wove my way through a curtain of cobwebs and spiritual enigmas which ultimately gave me a clearer understanding of the ways people relate to each other—on a family level and through the dynamics of living in times past and present, times in which religious institutions and the clergy impose a world view on believing minds. In addition to uncovering ghost stories, I learned family histories and the histories of New Mexican towns and attitudes; I encountered the impact of the relatively new Anglo culture upon the pre-established experience of the Native American and the Hispanic.

Furthermore, I wondered how my readers would react to some of the stories. I was curious if I would be taken seriously by non-believers, or conversely, if I would offend the believers. After grappling with these considerations for several days, I decided to forge ahead with the task of compiling the research for the book.

One of the major motivating factors in completing this project was my discovery that no book currently exists on the subject of Santa Fe or Taos ghosts. This omission surprised me because both locations have a well-known reputation for supernatural occurrences among their native population.

My interviews provided me with the eye-opening experience of witnessing the after-effects of encounters with the weird, eerie, spooky, and at times, evil. My childhood experiences taught me to be sensitive to unexplainable yet real examples of a life beyond the tangible. In my family, we did not make fun of such subjects as ghosts, hauntings, or brushes with the supernatural. Quite the contrary, my mother taught us to maintain a cautious respect for spirits, folk healers, witches, and forces considered to be occult in origin. Undoubtedly, my Mescalero Apache grandfather, who was brought to Santa Fe as a child to be "educated" at the Indian

School, provided his daughter, my mother, with the basis for such a positive and respectful view of the paranormal.

My parents were healers who were able to draw upon the afterdeath sphere. As a child, I accompanied them on their frequent visits to households blemished by the misfortunes of illness or the troubles of misguided spirits. Through this personal apprenticeship, I came to witness both the positive and negative aspects of spirits. The most important learning factors I acquired from my family experience were understanding and respect for the spirits and their energies.

However, my personal perplexities on the subject of ghosts presented an additional hurdle: Would the individuals—the Native Americans, Hispanics, seniors and religiously pious I chose to interview-grant me the privilege? I decided at the onset of the project to maintain respect for the personal thoughts and beliefs of each person interviewed; furthermore, I decided that if there was ever a time during any interview when I felt I might be crossing the border of sensitivity, cultural or otherwise, I would not press the issue. Happily, my own Native American background (Otomi, Mescalero Apache) afforded me the instinctive moral and intellectual understanding to recognize when I was about to enter another person's "space."

During my interviews with the area's residents, occasionally, I touched upon intimate topics such as family structures, love relationships, money, religious attitudes, and personal definitions of death and afterlife. I was repeatedly surprised at the ease with which people discussed their experiences. Although some people were understandably hesitant, overall I met with little resistance. The people I interviewed were not unusual or particularly exceptional in their spiritual or religious capacities. They represent a cross-section of city folk: nurses, janitors, administrators, laborers, and professionals. Some could trace their family roots in Santa Fe and Taos four or more generations back. In addition, I interviewed several Pueblo Native Americans, and contrary to popular beliefs, it is not necessarily true that Native Americans will not discuss stories of ghosts. However, it does not hurt to know the culture's rules of decorum, both spoken and unspoken. I am convinced that my sensitivity and personal knowledge of Native American culture was a definite asset.

I learned that people are both fascinated and very serious about the subject of ghosts. At this point, I must emphasize that the stories contained within these pages are not intended simply to amuse. They are not fanciful tales to be recounted on stormy nights to groups of wide-eyed Boy Scouts. The people who confided their personal experiences to me deserve courteous respect. They remain confident and secure in the knowledge that they are not conjuring up experiences of their own imaginations; instead, they maintain with personal honesty that their experiences truly happened. In addition, not only did these events happen, they may happen again—to you. Whenever possible, I have given detailed descriptions of the places where these events occurred. You are welcome to locate these places, but please *respect the privacy and property of the inhabitants/informants*. Please use common sense and discretion.

I find it personally gratifying to know that amid the silver and turquoise shops, the vendors, the upscale art galleries and the posh restaurants, deep within the earthen walls of these ancient cities, the souls of the dead refuse to be forgotten.

The interviews required a considerable amount of editing. As anyone knows who has conducted interviews by transcribing from tape recordings to the written page, the process is not as simple as it might appear. careful attention must be paid in order to keep the right "feeling" of the interview. Arranging and giving the proper emphasis where it was obvious, keeping the subject matter in context, attempting to describe facial expressions and hand gestures, among other human characteristics, can be challenging, but is not impossible. I attempted to keep the narrative flow and the mental image of the interview as close to genuine as possible. I must confess, however, sometimes I needed to change a sentence here for the story to proceed smoothly and be understood clearly. This editing was necessary, but does not detract from the story's principal subject matter. The stories speak for themselves.

The stories, I believe provide more questions than answers to thoughts the reader might have about the existence of ghosts. For example: What is a ghost? Do ghosts harm or do they provide a positive direction for the living? Can a ghost be an angel, fallen or otherwise? Do animals have spirits? Enduring questions are raised about how we as human beings see ourselves and how we interpret life and death.

It would be presumptuous for me or anyone else, for that matter, to claim to have the answers for or against the existence of ghosts. Culturally, what is our focus regarding death, and how does this cultural view differ from our personal view? Death can be dirty, at times it is messy. In western nations death is assigned to a profession of licensed artists known as morticians. Their attempts to keep death clean and to make the dead look as lifelike as possible is all in vain. Ultimately, death wins over. Death is patient, death can be kind. It can end pain, it can cause much pain. Death can change the course of history. Above all, death must be respected. The twin sister of life is death. Death welcomes you no matter whom or what you believe in, how much money you make, or what color you are. Death is an equal opportunity provider. Given all this, where do ghosts fit into the web of death? Perhaps these questions can be answered only through our customs and traditions. Then again, perhaps not.

Ghosts offer the living, not only curious and sometimes strange fodder for stories and folklore, but also insight into another world in which time and space cease to exist. These samples of stories will provide the reader with engaging reading and a bit of a history lesson as well.

The stories of the ghosts of New Mexico will forever remain unfinished. We owe it to ourselves to listen with our hearts, to reach across time and to hear the voices of what will one day be ourselves.

Death may be eternal, but life is not. Let's treat each other as the precious spirits we truly are.

Antonio R. Garcez

ADOBE ANGELS
THE GHOSTS OF SANTA FE AND TAOS

Introduction

Both Santa Fe and Taos are particularly interesting cities. Many beings have left their spiritual mark on their soils. Be they Native Americans, "Children of the Sun" from Mexico, Spanish explorers, or, most recently, the descendants of European Caucasians. They have all shaped the landscape and the traditions of these mud-walled cities. Visitors experience the awe-inspiring culture of the Southwest, witness first-hand the landscape Georgia O'Keeffe set to canvas, wonder at the unique adobe architec-

ture, and savor the flavors and aromas of the Northern New Mexico cuisine. Most, however, rarely share one of the most interesting aspects of these cities—the inhabitants who once were, yet continue to be, important parts of the community—the ghosts.

Non-believers regard stories of first-hand experiences with the supernatural as "amusing" and "colorful" figments of the imagination of the "primitive" mind. The truth is that our ghosts continuously entice us to view them through the transparent, misty glass of another time, one that presents the viewer with a panorama of veiled shadows, screaming night dogs with human faces, whispering owls that call out the names of those who pass, arms of hatred that enclose the innocent and the weak, or cold winds that cause the skin to crawl and stenches of coffin air to envelope the mind.

Ghosts continuously make their presences known throughout Santa Fe and Taos, some in a positive manner, others through evil and sinister manifestations. In New Mexico, as in communities throughout the world, sincere and saintly healers, when called upon, confront and sometimes battle these spiritual foes. Ghosts can be manipulated to do the bidding of the living either to cause harm or to direct goodness. In this book, you will read true stories of such encounters. You will read of the fierce wind that drove a demon through one family's living room window; you will read of the young man so involved with Satanism he killed a neighbor's dog and then committed suicide. But, at the opposite end of the spectrum, you will read of spirits who traverse the night hallways of popular hotels and want nothing more than to be acknowledged and recognized. Further, you will read of a woman's spirit that wanders the banks of the Santa Fe River beseeching forgiveness for some ancient transgression.

The many picturesque sections of Santa Fe and Taos, their buildings, houses and thoroughfares where these past events occurred, still endure supernatural manifestations. Not all the past remnants of Santa Fe and Taos are in their museums. Perhaps symbolic of this is the singularly special sense of relation to another time, another experience, when men and women touched their spiritual selves by acknowledging the predictable force that is the twin of life—death, made evident by the hardships and struggles of daily, earthly life.

At dusk, as the piñon and juniper wood smoke rises up the adobe chimneys of these ancient, high desert cities and as the cool night wind rustles through the leaves of the majestic cottonwoods, a distant, unfamiliar sound breaks the calm—the cry of terror, a scream that raises the body hairs, the piercing call that reaches into the soul and devours sanity.

Welcome to the abode of the ghosts of New Mexico. These stories are as real and as true as the people who relate them. These stories speak for themselves.

Sister George

Sister Harold (L) and Sister Miriam George Simon (R) with students of the Santa Fe Opportunity School, 1948.

History

The Three Sisters Boutique, 211 Old Santa Fe Trail, Santa Fe, New Mexico, has a well-known reputation for strange goings-on. Presently, Ms June Keys owns the store which specializes in western wear "a la Santa Fe." Ms Keys is one of the many inhabitants who have experienced, first-hand, the benevolent manifestations of Sister George's ghost.

Several decades ago, on the site of the boutique, Sister George, along with several other nuns, ran a school for physically and mentally challenged children of the city. The nuns belonged to the Catholic order known as the Sisters of Loretto. The members of this order were responsible for building the famous Loretto

Chapel, located in the heart of Santa Fe.

In 1970, the school closed and the building was sold to the Best Western Corporation. The corporation tore down the adobe school buildings except for a portion along Alameda Street, which had been used for various purposes—horse stable, chicken coop, storage area. At one time, this section of the original buildings housed the Opportunity School, co-directed by Sister Harold and Sister George.

The two nuns raised the needed finances for upkeep and supplies by organizing large community barbecues. Sister George also marshaled the help of the New Mexico State Penitentiary for the much-needed repair of the school's classroom floors. In addition, she was very active as a community networker and teacher. She cared for the children of the Opportunity School until a devastating fire destroyed the main school building in the late 1960's. A few years later, Sister George died.

Because of the historical and sentimental importance of the site, the new owners preserved two of the original structures— the beautiful Loretto Chapel and Sister George's Opportunity School building.

Early Apparitions

Once the hotel corporation built the Loretto Inn, the modest schoolhouse became a valuable piece of real estate and was leased as commercial property. The first business to occupy the schoolhouse was the Copy Company, owned by James Kirkpatrick. One of his employees, Blue Rogers, who did everything from building shelves and counters to painting, was the first person to experience the ghost of Sister George. Mr. Rogers has stated that he heard footsteps in empty rooms, he saw lights blink on and off without explanation, and the office machines would turn on and off by themselves. He also attests to the fact that large reams of office paper would be moved from their original positions in a matter of a few minutes.

It all came to a head one day when the owner announced in a disturbed and irritated voice, "Enough is enough!" There were no further disturbances for several months. Then, one night when Mr. Rogers was alone, working after hours at the rear of the store, he heard a woman singing in a pleasantly, high-pitched voice. The singing was soft and pealing like a bell. The sound seemed to be coming from the front of the store, and although he had carefully closed and locked the doors for the evening, Rogers decided to investigate. As he approached the front room, the singing ceased. He turned on the lights and saw nothing out of the ordinary, so he switched off the lights and made his way back to his work area.

A few minutes later, he heard the singing again. After two more fruitless investigations, Rogers decided to ignore the whole situation. The singing continued for a total of two hours.

There are several rooms in the building that were originally used as classrooms. Mr. Kirkpatrick's sisters-in-law rented these rooms and turned them into a variety shop called The Santa Fe Store. It was stocked with souvenirs and Santa Fe style clothing. The women have claimed that after hours, when the store was closed, they would hear the clothes hangers sliding along the metal racks—by themselves. Hangers with clothing on them would move back and forth on the racks, and the lights would switch on and off—in empty rooms.

Another strange incident at The Santa Fe Store occurred each morning during the first week of operations. When the two women checked their cash register, they invariably found an extra ten dollar bill that they could not account for. A nun from the Loretto Chapel theorized that it was Sister George giving the ladies her blessing. Since Sister George had been known as a "harvester" of donations, it was thought she could be making a contribution to help the new business get off the ground.

Recent Happenings

The following two interviews reveal detailed accounts of Sister George's current ghostly activities. The first interview is with Ms Keys, present co-owner of The Three Sisters Boutique, and the second is with a woman I will call "Melinda" who wishes to remain anonymous.

Sister "George"

Both stories leave no doubt about Sister George's desire to remain an important part of the present activities in "her" building. My guess is that she will continue to be a vital member of the Santa Fe community as she certainly had been in its past.

June Keys' Story

About two years ago, when I first opened the business, I experienced several strange occurrences. I always open up early and go directly to my office in the rear of building to begin the paperwork for the previous day's sales. One morning I recall feeling a "presence," as if someone had come into the store with me even though I was alone and had made sure I locked the door behind me. But the strong feeling that someone's eyes were staring at me was impossible to overcome. I felt uncomfortable. This is how my experience with Sister George's ghost began.

A few days later, after an extremely busy day, I went to the storeroom, located in the rear, to unpack some new clothes and arrange them on a wooden frame I used as a clothes rack. I had found the frame, which I guess had been an old classroom chalk board, under some cardboard boxes and debris in the storeroom. After I cleaned it up, I decided it would make a nice, temporary clothes rack.

I've been in the retail clothing business for several years, and have adopted my own way of doing things. One fanatical habit I have is to hang clothes on racks with the hangers facing the wall. I have been hanging clothes in this manner for years; it has become my personal style. Well, the following morning, when I came to the store, I decided to move the new clothes I had hung on the rack in the storeroom to an empty clothes rack in the showroom. When I entered the storeroom, I discovered that all the clothes and hangers I had painstakingly arranged on the wooden rack the night before had been reversed.

I became very upset, thinking that someone had entered the store and gone through the clothing. When my assistant arrived, I questioned her, but she assured me that she had not been in the store since the previous day and had certainly not moved the clothes. Now I was bewildered.

A few days later, a strange incident happened involving some customers. Separately, several women entered the dressing room and immediately came out, saying that they had the feeling someone was watching them or that someone was in the small dressing room with them. One woman returned to the counter with

Ms. June Keys, owner of The Three Sisters Boutique.

her blouse, told me of her fright, and showed me her arms—covered with goose bumps. Needless to day, she was no longer in a mood for shopping.

I have had no further incidents regarding what I believe is the ghost of Sister George. The spirit has never hurt anyone. I believe that she makes her presence known only to keep us aware that she had put a lot of time and love into her school and to remind us of her good works in the city and especially for the children.

Melinda's Story

Several years ago, when I worked at The Santa Fe Store, I had an experience that made me believe, without question, in the existence of ghosts. I have not discussed the experience with any-

The Three Sisters Boutique

one for more than a year because I was afraid to recall the whole thing. It was something I did not welcome and do not wish to experience again.

One morning about 8:00 a.m., I was in the back room, the storeroom of the store. I was arranging various boxes on the shelves when I heard the sound of footsteps in the showroom. I thought at first it was a delivery boy, but I realized that I had locked the door behind me when I entered. I decided to see what was going on.

I took one step into the well-lit showroom and noticed a rack of clothes at the far end move. The clothes swayed back and forth as I watched for a second or two. Then the whole rack, which was over six feet long and loaded with dresses and blouses, lifted on end and rose toward the ceiling. I stood, frozen with fright. The rack came back down then rose up again—three separate times.

Talk about cold chills and hot flashes—I was gripped with terror. I knew the doors and windows were closed. But even a strong gust of wind could not have lifted that rack and left everything else in the room undisturbed. And there was something else unusual—when the rack settled, after the third time, the clothes were absolutely still. They did not wiggle as one would expect, but came to a dead stop as if some unknown force held each stitch of clothing in place.

Even though I saw plainly that there was not another living soul in the small room, I decided to make sure. I gathered my courage and searched the room, pushing the clothes aside. I found no one hiding among the racks.

I must admit I was visibly shaken, and I was unable to speak to anyone about this incident. I quickly made my way to the front door and left for the remainder of the day. As I think back, I believe it was the ghost of Sister George. Maybe she was trying to get my attention or even playing with me. Soon after that incident, I leased the building and moved into another shop within the Loretto Inn compound, closer to the chapel.

Sister George: A Chronology

June 24, 1909	Born, Pirtleville, Arizona to George Simon and Miriam Shamas (Syrian for Simon); Both parents were Syrians and Catholics.
March 17, 1910	Baptized at Immaculate Conception Church, Douglas, Arizona.
August 14, 1931	Confirmed by Archbishop Daeger.
	Most of elementary and secondary education received in public school, Douglas, Arizona.
February, 1926	Entered the Loretto Community.
August 15, 1926	Received the habit of the Sisters of Loretto.
August 16, 1927	Took her first vows.

Teaching Assignments

1927	St. Francis Cathedral, Santa Fe, New Mexico.
1930	Our Lady of Sorrows, West Las Vegas, New Mexico.
1933	Loretto Academy, Las Cruces, New Mexico.
1935	St. Francis Cathedral, Santa Fe, New Mexico.
1940	Opportunity School, Santa Fe, New Mexico.
1970	Retired.
1975	Moved to Nazareth Hall, El Paso, Texas.

May 30, 1976 Died; 50th year of religious life.

Grant Corner Inn

In 1905 a colonial-styled home of the 'railroad era" was constructed on the corner of Johnson Street and Grant Avenue for a wealthy New Mexican ranching family named Winsor. The Winsors' lived in the home for a short time (possibly a year) before it was acquired by the First Presbyterian minister of Grant Avenue's church, Reverend Moore. Shortly thereafter, Reverend Moore passed away, leaving the house to his widow, Ada Peacock Moore, and their four children, Eta, Ada, Ruth and Mary.

Ada Peacock then married Arthur Robinson, well-known in Santa Fe for his spunk and eccentricities. The rumor goes that he was fired from his job at the post office for stealing stamps which earned him a jail sentence. Other stories include Arthur Robinson chasing children away from the house, stealing milk from Safeway, and maintaining a decorated Christmas tree in the window all year long! Ada helped the family income by teaching piano in what is now the bathroom in room number 8. Arthur (after his scrape with the law) miraculously became Justice of the Peace and maintained an office in what is currently Grant Corner Inn's office. Many Santa Feans reminisce about marriages in the parlor and payment of traffic fines in the office. Many of those residents remember the judge as being most fair with a jovial disposition. After Ada's death, the judge began to take in boarders. He also converted the back second-story porch into a "sleeping porch" where he slept. (This room is Grant Corner Inn's guest room number 4.)

After Judge Robinson's death in the 1950s, the house became "La Corte" Building, offering office space for lease. Each bedroom, as well as the living and dining rooms, became offices. Leroy Ramirez and Albert Gonzales, the new owners, had their offices in the building as well. The Chamber Music offices at one time occupied most of the rooms on the second floor.

In April, 1982 the Walter family purchased La Corte Building and moved from Phoenix to begin work on their Bed and Breakfast Inn. A nine-month renovation period included new plumbing and electrical wiring, a gazebo and picket fence with tree plantings, a new front roof line with new porch colonnades, and the addition of a downstairs commercial kitchen and outdoor back staircase and porch. The woodwork in the office, the banister and the mantel as well as all the wood floors were totally refurbished. Pat, a builder, and Louise, an interior designer, did much of the work on the house themselves. With the addition of their collections of art work and furnishings, the old house became a home again and opened as Grant Corner Inn December 15, 1982.

I interviewed Art Garcia at his home for this story. Surrounded by the well-appointed southwest furnishing of his home, he described to me his experience at the three story home which is now known as Grant Corner Inn. The unpleasantness of living through the events which he described still remains with Art. For instance, as Art described his series of ghostly encounters, his facial expression and voice tonality gave away an emotional level of character, that seemingly only a person who had directly witnessed and personally experienced the realm of ghosts could give. I'm doubtful that Art can ever totally forget his stay on the third floor of the house. But for now, Art is content to pursue the daily activities of life in Santa Fe, without dwelling too much on the past.

Grant Corner Inn

Art Garcia's Story

In 1980, I was just out of college and living in Seattle, Washington, when I decided to return to my home town, Santa Fe, New Mexico. Through personal contacts, I met the owners of a three-storied house on Grant Street. These folks offered me a job as custodian of the building, and for this, they provided me with the third floor for my living quarters. I moved into my new apartment during the month of March, and my mother and I began the arduous task of cleaning and dusting the entire house. It took us over three weeks to make the place spotless.

Eventually, the second floor was rented to some art students who used the bedrooms as storage and workspace. They rarely stayed more than a few hours at a time and always let me know when they were in the house. Both floors had telephones, so when they were in the house, either I called them or they called me—as a courtesy.

One evening I attended a function at a local college and did not arrive home until about 11:00 p.m. I walked up to the third floor, passing through the second floor, which was in total darkness. There was no sign of anyone in the whole house. Once in my place, I turned on the television set and made myself a snack.

Just as I finished my sandwich, I heard some stirring sounds that seemed to be coming from the floor below. I thought the noises were coming from outside, maybe from someone on the sidewalk, but soon the sounds increased in volume and took on a piercing, roaring quality. Then I thought it might be the art students, but I knew them and was certain they would not make such a commotion at such a late hour. Furthermore, they had never worked during the night.

After about ten minutes of listening to the sound of doors opening and slamming shut and large, heavy objects dropping on the floor, I had had enough. I telephoned the flat below to ask about the noise. The phone just rang and rang—I could even hear the ringing through the floor. When there was no answer, I decided it must be burglars, so I hung up the phone and switched off the television. From the third floor, there was no way out except through the second floor—or to jump—so I sat tight.

I then decided to call my father, and as I was describing the experience to him, the noises began again. But the sounds were now overhead, on the roof. The noise was deafening—constant pounding that reverberated throughout the third floor. My father said he'd be right over, so I hung up and listened to what sounded like someone walking on the roof. The footsteps were so loud that, when I made another call, I could not hear the voice at the other end of the telephone. Now the sounds were enveloping the entire third floor.

When the noise subsided some, I called my parents' home again. My mother told me that my father was on his way over. I telephoned the police and reported a burglary in progress. Soon I saw the flashing blue and red lights on a patrol car pulling up in front of the building. As I withdrew from the window and turned in the direction of the stairwell leading below, I smelled a faint, yet extremely foul, odor. The scent grew stronger until I had to place my hand over my mouth to keep from disgorging the contents of my stomach.

I made my way two steps down the stairwell when I heard the sound of a door on the second floor open and slam shut. I stopped, grabbed hold of the handrail, and peeked over to the floor below. I waited, expecting to see the police officer, but instead I heard the sound of footsteps approaching the stairs. The footsteps stopped and then suddenly began ascending the stairs—towards me. I stared into the sound but saw nothing. The footsteps were loud, and the sounds echoed off the walls. I froze.

All at once, I felt a cold, bone-chilling rush of air speed past me, followed by the over-powering stench of rotted meat. It smelled as if the large carcass of a decomposing animal with its entrails exposed and bubbling with the wrath of death were lying on the stairs below. This wafting, invisible fog of decay became stronger as each footstep approached me. Soon, it seemed as though the footsteps were just a few feet in front of me. Then suddenly something shoved my shoulder with tremendous force, as if pushing me out of the way.

I grabbed the banister to steady myself and then decided to make my escape. I ran down the stairs to the front door where I met the police—just about to ring the doorbell. The police entered and searched every room in the house. They discovered nothing. Soon my father arrived and helped me lock every door and window. Then he drove me to my parents' house where I spent the night.

The following day I returned to the house on Grant Street, but for my own peace of mind, I brought my parents along. We walked through the house together, checking everything. As I began the climb to the third floor, I noticed that all of the beautiful, large potted plants I had been caring for located on the stairs were completely wilted. I looked closer and realized that the leaves and stems had frozen. I was completely baffled. I had left several steam heaters on overnight, and the house was comfortably warm. In my bedroom, the large tropical plants now resembled defrosted frozen vegetables—limp and soggy. I searched throughout the third floor for a draft or some other source but found nothing.

That evening I turned the television on to watch a favorite comedy show. At approximately 11:00 p.m. again I heard movement on the floor below me. I immediately turned the television off. There was no doubt—the noises from the night before were back, but this time the sounds started up very quickly—as if in

Art Garcia

vengeance. Soon the sounds were deafening—the loud slamming of doors and pounding on the walls. I had to do something, so I phoned the police. I was not about to report a ghost, so I said that a burglar was in the house. As the noises reached a climax, I decided not to stay a minute longer. I made my way down the stairs and out the front door to my car. In the car, I felt safe. Once again I spent the night at my parents' home.

In the safety of my parents' living room, I phoned the police department and asked to speak to the officer who had responded to my burglary call. The officer informed me that, as he had approached the house, he saw blinking lights on both the first and second floors. Lights seemed to be moving rapidly from room to room as if someone were carrying them.

For five more nights, I attempted, with all of my will power, to spend a quiet, normal evening at home. But as soon as the eleventh hour struck, the slamming and pounding commenced. And once again I would take myself off to the comfort and safety of my parents' home.

My nerves were frayed, but I felt I had to prove to myself that I had some semblance of courage remaining. On the sixth night, I turned on all the lights on my floor and waited for the loathsome sounds—nothing happened. For a week after that, I experienced continued peace. But then, abruptly, the noises started up again, and I questioned my own sanity. I thought that I might be having a nervous breakdown. Maybe I was imagining the whole thing. I would lie awake at night for hours until my fatigued body would finally doze off.

Each morning it took all of the strength I could muster just to get out of bed. I would arrive at work with dark circles under my eyes. My co-workers and friends began inquiring about my health. At this point, I consulted a psychiatrist. The psychiatrist said I appeared to be under a tremendous amount of stress but that there was no pathological problem. He felt I was quite normal.

As the days and nights passed, I decided to get a housemate, and a short time later, two friends of mine moved in. Soon, we all began to see and hear unexplainable phenomena. Sometimes lights would turn off and on in empty rooms. At all hours of the day and night, we heard the sound of several human voices coming from the empty floor below. Often we heard loud laughter in empty rooms on our own floor. From the second floor, we heard the toilet flush and doors opening and closing. At times, the scent of a rancid, flowery perfume of preceded the unexplained sounds. Whenever I recall that odor, I still get goose bumps.

My brother, who at that time was a city police officer, visited me several times and personally witnessed these happenings. On the first and second floors, several times we actually saw a door knob turn and the door open, only to slam shut—all on its own.

On several occasions, my mother grabbed a door knob to open a door and felt the door being pulled away from her. However, my mother shouted, "You're not going to win this one!" Then she pulled with all her strength, using two hands, until the door gave. My roommates had similar experiences, but they were not as insistent in pursuing a ghostly tug of war.

One day by chance I met a couple in town who had lived in the house before I did. When they lived there, they had a young child. They told me that they had experienced similar phenomena. The unearthly experiences finally drove them to move out, and then a very strange thing happened. They began packing room by room. As they completed one room, neatly stacking the filled boxes, they moved on to another, but when they returned to the finished room, they found their boxes emptied and the contents strewn about the room.

Initially, my two housemates found the unusual incidents amusing; however, they soon grew tired of the situation and decided to seek other living quarters. The day they moved out another friend, Ken, and his cat Missie moved in.

On several occasions, Ken and I observed Missie walk into a room and then suddenly arch her back and hiss loudly at an invisible enemy. As every hair on her body and tail stood out straight, Missie backed her way out of the room. Ken and I looked at each other but said nothing.

At other times, I would put a record on the stereo, but soon the arm would be lifted off the record and the stereo turned off. Another time, when I was watching television one evening, a gust of wind suddenly and violently swung all the hanging plants and light fixtures. Loose papers flew in all directions. Then, as suddenly as it had begun, the wind ceased. I checked all the windows, but each was shut tight. I found no way that a wind with such force could have entered the room.

A new series of incidents began when I was taking a shower. I suddenly heard a woman's voice laughing loudly and harshly. I immediately parted the shower curtain and peeked out but saw nothing out of place. However, there was another time when I did see something out place. I had been asleep but was awakened by a noise in the bedroom. I slowly opened my eyes and saw a white shadowy figure moving along the wall. I did not move a muscle. I stared at the figure, and it began to laugh. It was the same laughter I had heard before while in the shower. The figure laughed but made no movement within its form. Then the laughter suddenly turned to crying, and the figure moved closer to my bed. As it stood next to my bed, it slowly dissolved until it had totally vanished. But, as soon as it disappeared, I felt the mattress at the foot of the bed depress as if someone were sitting down on it. I grabbed the blankets and covered my head. My heart was pounding hard in my chest. This was more frightening than anything I had experienced before.

Not long after that experience, I received a call from a priest from the local Guadalupe parish. He said my aunt, Ruby Sandoval, had discussed my situation with him and had asked him to talk with me because she was concerned for my safety. I agreed to meet him and he agreed to keep our conversation in strictest confidence.

When I met the priest, I was surprised as to how young he was. He began by asking me questions about my personal beliefs and whether I had ever studied or was interested in demonology, Satanism, witchcraft, or the occult. I told him no, and then he questioned me about the events I had experienced in the house on Grant Street. I told him everything, and at the close of our visit he said he would like to conduct a blessing at the house. I had no problems with his suggestion and agreed to an appointment on the following evening.

At work the next day, I described my meeting with the priest to a co-worker, Jean. When she heard about the happenings at the house and the planned blessing, she asked to be present, as a witness. I agreed, and that evening both Jean and I sat in the bedroom awaiting the priest.

    We didn't have long to wait, for soon a car pulled up. The priest had arrived. We hurried downstairs and met him as he was walking up the front porch steps. As soon as he entered my apartment, he began dressing for the ceremony, putting on his chasuble and vestment stole. Next he brought out holy water and began sprinkling the room. The moment he sprinkled the water towards the living room wall, we heard a loud cracking sound like splitting wood followed by a loud bang. Jean and I looked at each other, not masking our astonishment and fear. I felt as if I was in a movie. The priest performed the blessing, moving solemnly from room to room throughout the entire house—from attic to basement.

    Since the night of the blessing, I have had no more negative experiences with slamming doors, poundings on the walls, or rotten odors. I became convinced that the blessing had removed or quieted whatever had been in the house. I enjoyed the peace that prevailed throughout the house.

    Several weeks later, I left for the west coast, and my parents assumed the task of checking on the empty house on Grant Street. Each night between 9:00 and 10:00 pm, they drove by the building to make certain all was well.

    When I returned, I contacted my parents and asked about the welfare of the building. My mother's voice became quite concerned as she described what they had seen. On several occasions, as they drove by the house, they saw the figure of a man standing in one of the windows on the third floor. He seemed to be staring at the street. One time, my parents called my brother, a police officer, and he too saw the figure. When my brother arrived, they all entered the building to investigate, but found no one there and nothing out of place. All the doors and windows were locked.

    About three weeks after I returned from my trip, a woman who claimed to be a clairvoyant visited me. She just knocked on my door one day, and after she told me of her "world renowned" history as a medium, I invited her in. As soon as she entered the building, she said she felt vibrations.

    I led her to the first floor living room and we sat down.

    She began to breath slowly and deeply. Then she paused and,

with closed eyes, began describing people she identified as lost souls existing in the house. She said she was seeing two female figures and a male figure standing off to one side, observing things. Of the two females, the older appeared to be angry because of her actions and movements. The clairvoyant said that she could not understand what the younger woman and the man were saying, but the older woman told her that she had been trapped on the second floor—no matter what she did she could not free herself from that floor. Soon, the clairvoyant opened her eyes and told me that the spirits need help in order to understand that they must go on with the process of death. She said they were reliving their past lives with much energy. However, the clairvoyant left and never returned. I have had no further contact from her.

For days, I continued to dwell on what the clairvoyant had told me, and finally I decided to move out of the house. I gathered boxes and packed my belongings. I stacked the boxes in the middle of the bedroom and went to get some lunch. A few minutes later, when I returned, I found the boxes opened and the contents tossed about the room—except for my books. They had been neatly stacked into small piles on the floor beside the empty boxes. I recalled the experience of the former family as they tried to leave the house, and I became even more determined to move. I found a place and settled on the west side of Santa Fe where I live now.

Some years later, I learned something very interesting about the original owners of the house on Grant Street. The husband was a postal worker, and he kept his wife, a paraplegic, on the second floor. I cannot verify the accuracy of this information, but it does coincide with what the clairvoyant had said. I also learned that the adult daughter, who had lived in the house until the 1970's, was killed with her husband in an automobile accident.

Since the day I moved out, I never returned to that house. I have no desire to go back. The memories of my experiences there remain very fresh in my mind. I am pleased that the present owners transformed the house into a luxurious bed and breakfast because it was a beautiful home, and now it is even more special. Along with my memories, I frequently dream about the time I lived there, and I constantly live with the fear of knowing that someone or something is watching me.

Doña Leticia

One hot August day, I interviewed Alberto Serna. We sat on his front porch, and as we talked, Daniel, Alberto's seventeen year old son, sat with us and listened intently to his father's story of Doña Leticia, a witch. Frequently, Alberto would pause and reflect upon other memories awakened as he related his story. At these times, Daniel would ask his father to explain further, to provide small details of these family memories. I enjoyed those moments and appreciated being present as an oral tradition was transferred from one generation to another.

Now in his fifties, Alberto related a brief incident which occurred six years before when he returned to his old neighborhood. On that day, in place of the former homes of his neighbors —including Doña Leticia's house—he found scattered bushes of Chamisa and dust. But as he walked back to his car, he spotted a large, black raven standing on a boulder. It cawed several times then abruptly lifted off and flew away.

When I asked Alberto what he took this to mean, he answered, "I know it was just that old witch letting me know she's still around—to this very day!"

Alberto Sena's Story

My name is Alberto Serna, and I am the oldest of four brothers. My family and I once lived in a little settlement three miles northeast of Santa Fe. My grandfather had built our home of adobe in 1918, and when he died in 1953, he passed it to my mother who already had a growing family. This home, along with Doña Leticia's house, was demolished soon after the family sold the land to the New Mexico Highway Department. Presently, I live on the west side of Santa Fe and have two sons.

As a child of fifteen, I had already learned of ghosts and witches through the stories passed from one generation to the next, including stories of the famous La Llorona. So when my father took me aside and told me of Doña Leticia, a neighbor who lived about a quarter of a mile east of our home, I was not surprised by my father's lecture. He warned me to avoid the old spinster and stay away from her home. When I asked why, he replied simply, *"Es una bruja"* [She is a witch.]

He told me that he had always suspected her but hadn't any proof until his friend Juan told him how Doña Leticia had given his brother *el mal ojo* [the evil eye]. My father said that soon Juan's brother became bedridden and remained that way for a month until his wife tearfully beseeched Doña Leticia and offered her cash to remove the spell.

I also learned that Doña Leticia had a small wooden box in which she kept some sort of animal that she could manipulate to work her magic. The witch fed the animal a concoction of herbs, threads from an intended victim's clothes or strands of hair, and drops of Leticia's own blood.

I listened intently to my father's words and promised never to go near the witch's house—never.

About a month later, neighbors received the news that, while en route to Albuquerque with a close friend, Doña Leticia's cart had turned over and she had broken her back. She died the following day.

Because my parents were held in high regard in our community, Doña Leticia's only surviving relative, a seventy-three year old brother from Taos, gave them the opportunity to buy Doña Leticia's house and land for a reduced price. None of the neighbors wanted anything to do with the place, so, because my parents had saved up a few extra dollars, they purchased Doña Leticia's small homestead with the intention of fixing it up and renting it.

Once Doña Leticia's brother had removed most of her belongings and left for Taos, my parents and I entered the house. Apparently, in his haste, the brother had disturbed a floor board in the bedroom. I removed the board and found a small wooden box painted in a faded green patina. I retrieved the box and undid the tight twine holding the lid in place. The inside of the box was lined in red cloth and lying on the cloth was a black, coiled and shriveled worm. I assumed that this was the animal my father had told me about.

When I showed the box to my parents, my mother immediately made the sign of the cross and harshly instructed me to "Take that thing outside!" My father followed me out of the house and around to the back. Then he gathered some old boards which were lying in the yard and built a fire. Once the fire was roaring, he threw the box into the flames. I watched the passion of the fire consume the green box and its twisted, black contents.

Many months later, after painting, fixing the plumbing, and sprucing up the property, my parents finally rented the house to an older couple from Colorado. For the first few days, they seemed to be enjoying the place, but within two weeks they moved out. The woman said she was being bothered by nightmares.

Just a few days later, a group of family members and friends from the Chama area came to visit, so my mother offered to put them up at our house while my brothers and I slept in Doña Leticia's house.

That night, we went off to the old witch's house, knowing my father would join us later. We spent the early part of the evening listening to an old radio, but as the night grew darker, I heard a soft crying sound coming from the bedroom. I lowered the volume on the radio to hear better, and we all clearly heard the sound of a baby crying in the bedroom. As I got up to investigate, I saw on the wall of the hallway the shadows of three tall cats—standing upright. As I approached the shadows, they glided across the wall. I stood still. Then I heard what seemed to be an argument among the cats. They were speaking in women's voices. I ran back to the living room, grabbed my brothers' hands and dashed home.

I was shaking and sobbing when I reached the house and told my mother, in front of all our visitors, what I had experienced. My father, his brother and godfather decided to spend the night at the old woman's house.

Later that night, I was awakened by my father's voice. Then he and my mother grabbed blankets—one of mine—and set the men up on the floor of our house.

In the morning, my father told me the whole story. He said that the three men were joking and preparing their beds when they heard what sounded like a large dog scratching at the front door. My father opened the door slightly but saw nothing; however, as he turned toward the other men, something streaked into the house through the partially opened door. All three men saw a flash of black, head for the bedroom. As they followed it, they suddenly heard the loud, piercing scream of a woman.

"Fuera de mi casa. Fuera de mi casa!" [Out of my house . . .], she yelled.

Then the men saw the dark shadowy figure of a woman materialize and approach them as a cold rush of air pushed them out of the bedroom. They all scrambled out the front door and ran to our house, and that's when my father's voice woke me up.

Since that night, our family only ventured to Doña Leticia's house during the day. Unable and unwilling to use the house for family, my parents have rented it several times throughout the years, but inevitably the renters would leave, citing strange happenings or claiming that they saw or heard an unknown woman in the house.

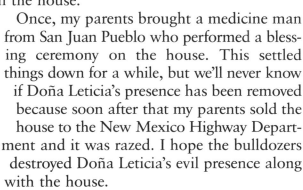

Once, my parents brought a medicine man from San Juan Pueblo who performed a blessing ceremony on the house. This settled things down for a while, but we'll never know if Doña Leticia's presence has been removed because soon after that my parents sold the house to the New Mexico Highway Department and it was razed. I hope the bulldozers destroyed Doña Leticia's evil presence along with the house.

The House on Apodaca Hill

When I consider the stories of the people I interviewed for this book, I believe that this particular interview with Ms Patricia Camacho will prove to be the most puzzling for the reader because of the overt malevolence and the down-right tenacious nature of the ghost(s). Ms Camacho presented her story in a calm manner, never giving an emotional reaction to the bizarre atmosphere surrounding what she, her family and friends experienced at 507 Apodaca Hill.

Stranger still—and most difficult to understand—is why she remains in this house. The mischievous incidents continue to this day. Experiencing just one sample of what Ms Camacho goes through would send most people packing in a matter of minutes. Apparently, Ms Camacho is a breed of woman who will stand her ground rather than forfeit her courage.

Patricia, it is my hope that you succeed.

507 Apodaca Hill

Patricia's Story

The house I am presently renting is over 70 years old. The landlord told me that it used to be a brothel and an illegal gambling hall in the 1920's. The house is divided into two sections with the bedrooms below ground level and the kitchen and living room above. The upper section was added in the 1950's and solidly constructed of adobe bricks in the Pueblo style, which is very distinctive of Santa Fe.

Patricia Camacho

Within the first few days of moving in—about three years ago—I had many separate and unusual experiences. One time, when I was walking down the stairs to my bedroom, I suddenly felt a hand grab my ankle, trying to trip me on the stairs. I actually felt a large hand hold tight to my ankle. This sensation disappeared as soon as I struggled free.

Several days later I was not so fortunate, and in the following weeks, I took many falls. My legs and arms became bruised from these falls. During these weeks, I also experienced nights when I was awakened by the touch of fingers on my face—this also happened in the daytime. As I was going about my house cleaning, I often felt something brush against my face. At first, I thought it was a bit of feather or a strand of spider web that was floating freely in the air and had landed on my face, but a look in the mirror revealed nothing.

Soon, the pressure of what was brushing against my face increased, and strands of my own hair would be lifted up into the air. It felt as if an invisible hand was caressing my face and fondling my hair. This continued for several days and nights, but I just shook my head and tried to go about my business.

There were also evenings when I was sitting up in bed reading and I noticed movement at the foot of the bed. I saw and felt the blankets slide across my feet and then saw the impression of a body sitting down on the bed. The mattress actually depressed with the circular impression of someone's behind on the comforter. As I slowly lifted the blankets to get out of bed, I clearly saw the mattress puff up, returning to its original form.

About two months ago, I was awakened in the middle of the night by my dog Miko's barking. As I awoke, I heard the loud pounding noise of someone hitting the wall area beside my head...then the whole bed shook as if someone wanted me out of bed. Miko growled and ran to the door to be let out.

Another strange phenomenon is the appearance of "cold spots" in several areas of the house. As I walk from one room to another, I often pass through an area of extreme cold, much colder than the surrounding temperature of the room I happen to be in. It seems as if there is a long vertical tube of frigid air that I pass through without notice—until I am in it.

II

These things happened within the first few months after I moved into the house, but as the months progressed, things took

"Miko"

a new approach. During the night, I would be awakened by a variety of noises. I would open my eyes and gaze at the darkened ceiling, listening to the sounds of bottles being moved about and of voices of people deep in conversation. The sounds seemed to be coming from the basement. I could detect the source of the sounds because the house is not very large and I am familiar with the rooms.

Most nights the voices sounded like a group of people, but on some nights, I was wakened by the voice of a man speaking very harshly and the sound of a woman responding loudly. It was difficult to make out what they were saying even though the language was English. The voices were muffled, but the intensity and the anger was very clear. I heard these voices only at night, but both night and day I heard the sounds of bottles being moved and sometimes broken.

Sometimes, when I was in one room like the kitchen, I would hear the sound of a breaking plate or vase coming from another room. At this, my dog would run in circles and bark wildly; then, I would run into the room expecting to see a mess of pottery on the floor. I would find only my dog, and I would have to let her out immediately, because of her extreme nervousness...

These smashing sounds could occur in any room at any time throughout the house. People who have spent the night with me have reported hearing the sounds of breaking glass and feeling both the extreme cold and the web-like fingers brush against their skin. One visitor heard the sound of someone chopping wood at 3:00 a.m. Other visitors reported seeing framed pictures lift off their nails and crash on the floor, articles of clothing move about or disappear, and jewelry or coffee cups disappear at the turn of a head.

One day, a friend, who was enjoying a hot cup of coffee in the living room, rose from her chair and left the room for a moment. When she returned, the cup was gone. To this day we have not found the cup. Friends and family, who have spent the night, awake in the morning and reach for their clothing only to find a shirt, or a shoe, or a sock missing.

III

My son Chris visited me on two occasions, and both times he lost items of clothing. The first time, during the summer, he slept on the couch in the living room for three nights. He said that each night he felt a touch on his face or on his leg. On the last night of his stay, he just could not take it anymore. He was awakened by the feeling of being shaken violently and the sound of a man's voice yelling at him, demanding he get up and go to church. Chris was caught off guard by this experience but got a good look at an older man with long blond or grey colored hair and a moustache. This man was wearing dark clothes and soon disappeared. After that experience, my son returned to his own home.

Several months later, Chris came for another overnight stay. It was Christmas time, so I guess he felt compelled to spend a few nights—ghost or not. Each morning he told me of his unusual experiences. On the first two nights, he felt extremely cold gusts of air moving past him, and he heard a noise that he described as a bottle rolling on the floor. Not much else happened, so he began to relax.

However, during the last night of his stay, all hell broke loose. I was making my way downstairs to one of the bedrooms, and my son was watching television in the living room with my dog at his side. All of a sudden, we heard a tremendous sound of breaking glass and furniture being thrown about in the bedrooms. My dog began howling and ran to the basement. My son and I remained in our places, motionless. Then the dog's bark changed; she began barking as if someone were attacking her. Before I took one step down the stairs, the dog ran back upstairs and began running in circles. My son said he had had enough and went to a motel.

Ten minutes after my son left the house, the sounds started up again. As usual, when I went to the bedrooms to investigate, I found nothing broken or disturbed. The only evidence to suggest that someone had been in the rooms was the strong, musky scent of a man's cologne.

IV

My friend Jonathan, who visits often from Cochiti Pueblo, has heard the now-common noises emanating from the basement. (Jonathan's story follows.) He reports hearing a high-pitched woman's voice screaming at someone to leave her alone and the response of a man's voice, which Jonathan cannot clearly make out. Jonathan has also heard the sounds of furniture being thrown against the walls.

One night he was awakened by having his mattress shaken violently. When he opened his eyes and sat up, a loud thumping commenced on the wall next to his head. A Native American, Jonathan wears his hair long. He has told me that he has felt an invisible hand stroking his hair, and several strands have lifted up into the air by themselves. At these times, Jonathan has distinctly felt a presence standing beside him.

V

Another friend, Joe, from Taos Pueblo, who is a medicine man, visited me and immediately said, "You've got something very bad in this house, Patricia."

Joe's son, Standing Deer, who was with him, said that he felt covered in a cold chill and felt hands touching him.

Joe proceeded to make a small medicine bag for me, which I now carry at all times. Joe also burned sage incense and blessed the house to clear it of its bad spirits. For a few months after that, I had no problems.

But, not long after Joe's visit, a woman friend came from California to spend a week with me. One afternoon she was standing in the living room while I was in the kitchen. We were conversing between the rooms when, suddenly, she did not answer. I turned toward her and saw that her eyes were as large and as round as saucers. She stood there motionless, gazing at me as if she were in shock.

Then she yelled, "Oh my God! Someone is touching me!"

I went up to her and grabbed her arm. Her skin was ice cold, and her arms were covered in goose bumps. Because of my own experiences, I knew what was happening. I spoke loudly to her, attempting to break through the fright and horror. She responded in a shaky voice.

She said that a coldness had approached her and enveloped her, petrifying her senses. Very quickly the coldness had entered her body and soon she became hysterical, pleading with me to make the "thing" leave her alone. I hugged her and tried to settle her down. I told her to extend her hands palms up, and I held my hands over hers—palms down. Then I concentrated and demanded that whatever was taking over her body leave her. Soon after that, I felt the cold chill creep from my fingertips up my arms and throughout my body. Seconds later, the coldness left me and we hugged each other again.

At times I have considered seeking the help of a medium, perhaps to perform an exorcism, but I just haven't gotten around to it. A recent incident, however, may have convinced me. I was sitting at the kitchen table mulling over some thoughts, when suddenly one of the lower cabinet doors swung open and a glass baking dish flew out. I watched as the dish sped across the floor and hit the opposite wall with a tremendous crash, sending shards of glass in all directions. The sight was mentally staggering. I could not imagine how the door had opened or the dish had flown out. The dish had been set on the lower shelf of the cabinet. Immediately after the dish shattered, my dog began barking and ran to the front door to be let out.

I felt it was time to find out more about this house, so I asked my landlord Hank if he or his family had experienced anything unusual when they lived here. He told me his children had used the basement for their bedrooms, and they had placed a small television set on top of one of the dressers. He said that often the children would run upstairs shouting that a man had walked into the room and turned off the TV. Then this strange man simply walked into the wall and disappeared.

At other times, the children told of being awakened in the middle of the night by skeletons walking about on their beds. Like the strange man, the skeletons also disappeared through the wall. My landlord's oldest son corroborated these statements.

Hank told me that he too had heard loud noises, felt the cold spots throughout the house, and had "lost" various items.

Just two nights ago, while sitting in the upstairs living room, Miko started barking, ran to the bedroom, and jumped up on my bed. She continued barking, facing the wall where my pillow is. I saw nothing unusual. Then she stopped barking and just stared at the wall—as though she did not want to miss anything that might happen. Suddenly she began to bark uncontrollably, and try as I might, I could not stop her. Then she dashed to the living room door and scratched to be let out. She spent the remainder of the night outside, refusing to enter the house.

Well, I'm not sure what to do. Considering all that has taken place, I guess I'm quite lucky to be in one piece. I'll just stay where I am for the time being. I enjoy the house and the neighborhood, so a ghost or two is not going to make me start looking for a new place any time soon.

Jonathan's Story

Jonathan Loretto is a young man from the Cochiti pueblo, about twenty miles south of Santa Fe. He designs and produces stunningly beautiful pieces of silver and turquoise jewelry. Jonathan related the following story of his personal experience in the home of Patricia Camacho, where he maintains a workbench and jewelry-making studio in the basement. He believes the spirits he encountered intended no harm. You be the judge.

Patricia Camacho and I have been good friends for a long time, so when she offered her basement area for me to use as a workshop, I jumped at the chance. Although I did not at first notice anything out of the ordinary, Patricia informed me that there might be some strange noises or goings-on. But I was not expecting anything major—or scary—to happen.

About a year ago, I was down in the basement working on a delicate, woman's silver ring when I felt a presence in the room. I turned away from my work and glanced around the room, thinking that it might be Patricia paying me a visit. I saw no one so I went back to work.

A few minutes later, I felt the pressure of a hand caressing the back of my head. Immediately, I stopped working and sat motionless on my chair. I knew no one was in the room. Tied loosely with a strand of yarn, my long hair hung down my back. As I sat there, I again felt the pressure of a hand on my hair, and then I felt—and saw—some strands of my hair rise up into the air as if someone were lifting them.

Quickly, I stood up and moved away from the workbench, but again strands of my hair floated up. I waved my right hand, attempting to slap what was teasing me. Then I ran toward the stairs leading to the living room. Half way up the stairs, I felt something grab hold of a large mass of my hair and jerk my head backwards. Without a moment's thought I pulled away and quickly made my way up the stairs, to the living room and out the door! I waited outside until Patricia drove up to the house and saw me standing by the fence.

When I told Patricia of my experience, she admitted that other visitors had been similarly accosted.

Since that night, I have had second thoughts about working in the basement, but I have tried to put them aside. Then one day, I had been working and stopped to go upstairs for a drink. As I made my way back down the basement stairs, I suddenly felt a chilling coldness descend on me, and I clearly heard the sound of loud, harsh laughter. It was the laughter of a mad, hysterical woman, and it was coming from the basement. I ran back upstairs and outside to the comfort of the warm afternoon sun.

A few minutes later, I returned to the house but decided to stay in the living room and watch television—something to distract me. But as I sat on the couch, I again felt the cold chill and knew someone—or something—was in the room with me. The curtains were drawn open, filling the room with daylight. I looked in the direction where I thought the presence was and distinctly saw one of the couch cushions slowly depress...as if someone were sitting down on it. That was all I needed...I jumped up, did an "about face," and headed for the door.

Another curious incident happened when I spent the night at the house. I had removed my favorite "L. A. Raiders" tee shirt and draped it over a nearby chair then went to sleep on the couch. The next morning, I reached for the shirt, but it was gone. I searched everywhere. There had been no visitors, and I had personally locked the doors. The shirt was never found.

These days, I stay in the house only when someone else is there. I do not think the spirits are going to kill anyone...perhaps they just want to make an impression.

Guadalupe and La Llorona

Guadalupe was born to a family consisting of her parents and five older brothers. Because of the harsh conditions of rural life in the 1920's and the lack of proper medical care, three of her brothers had died by the time she celebrated her eighth birthday.

At the time of this interview, Guadalupe was seventy years old and in good health. She told me of many childhood experiences in Santa Fe, and she described the difficulties of daily existence without the aid of a telephone, automobile, or washing machine. As of seven years ago, Guadalupe was still practicing her "gifts" as *curandera* [healer] and midwife. To this day, the elder Hispanic people of the city seek her counsel. During my interview, we sat in her kitchen sipping coffee.

Guadalupe clasped her hands daintily in her lap and closed her hazel eyes in concentration, accenting the tiny wrinkles of her face. Then she told the story of her encounter with one of New Mexico's most famous spirits, *la llorona* [the weeping woman].

Guadalupe's Story

It happened one hot day in 1931 when I went with my brothers and a few neighborhood friends to the Santa Fe river. Even though it was four miles away, we didn't mind the walk because it would end in refreshment at the cool river. Before leaving, I gathered up my white puppy, who had been resting in the shade of a *piñon* tree and then ran to catch up with the others.

When we reached the river, my brothers began throwing small stones into the swirling eddies. I put my "peewee" ball of fur on the ground and joined in the game. After a few minutes, the sun beating down on my exposed head made me nauseous and I sought shade under some nearby willow trees. My puppy joined me as I dug up the reddish brown mud from the water's edge to make "mud people." I fashioned the bodies of mud, used twigs for the arms and legs, leaves for dresses, and small, flat stones for boys' hats. I could see and hear my brothers and their friends laughing and carrying on, but I was content to play house with my mud dolls and my puppy. Suddenly, while I was arranging the dolls in a circle, a strong gust of wind enveloped me, and the surrounding cattails and bull rushes swayed violently. Then I heard the sound of bells making a sweet tinkling noise. Captivated by the ringing, I stopped playing and listened.

As I turned to tell my brothers about the bells, I saw that they too had noticed the sounds, for they were standing silently, gazing at the sky. The sound of the bells got louder and louder, and my puppy, who stood at my side, began barking, then ran off into a large clump of cattails. I tried to go after him but discovered that I could not move a muscle. I was mesmerized by the sound of the bells for at least a minute.

Then the tinkle of the bells subsided, and in the sudden silence, I heard a woman gently sobbing and calling, "*Mija, mija* [daughter, daughter]." Suddenly, I was able to move, so I stood up and called to my brothers. They rushed to my side and took me by the hand. From the feeling of fear that gripped me, I knew this was something evil. We all raced home.

I soon learned that my brothers and the other children had also heard the woman crying and beseeching. But to them she had called out, "*Mis hijos, mis hijos* [my sons, my sons]."

Once I was safe at home, I realized that I had lost my puppy, and I cried because I was certain it had drowned.

After we explained what had happened, my mother said we had done the right thing by leaving that place. She said that from what we told her, she believed something evil had happened. My parents decided to make a visit to the spot where we had heard the weeping. I was apprehensive about returning, but at the same time, I was anxious to find my puppy.

As my father was getting the horses ready, I heard my mother whisper to him, "*La llorona* [the weeping woman]."

When we arrived at the river, the sun was hanging heavy and tired in the western sky, and as we approached the river's edge, we all heard the woman's voice and felt the sense of urgency as she cried loudly for her children, *"Mis hijos, mis hijos."*

My father called out to her, "*¿Quien es. En donde estas. Que quieres?* [Who are you? Where are you? What do you want?]"

He received no reply, so my mother shouted, "*Deje a mis hijos solos, hija del demonio* [Leave my children alone, daughter of the devil]." Then she made the sign of the cross and called to us, "*Vamonos* [Let's go]." And off we went.

But in our haste, my mother's horse which she and I were riding, tripped, and I fell off into the mud, hands first. As both of my parents came to help me, one of my brothers shouted for us to look at the river. We all turned and saw the apparition of woman with her arms outstretched walking toward us.

The setting sun had cast a deep red, orange, gold glow on the river, and we clearly saw this woman walking on its surface. My father yelled for us to hurry, and we quickly made our way back home. As soon as we got back, my parents alerted the neighborhood to the danger at the river. They told everyone what we had witnessed and warned them to keep a close watch on their children.

Most people think *la llorona* makes her presence known only at night, but I am here to tell everyone that evil can chose any time to come forth. To this day, I clearly recall that phantom woman walking on the water and crying for her children.

Canyon Road

Before the coming of the conquistadores, Canyon Road was already a well-traveled trail. Used by Native Americans of the Rio Grande Valley, it was the principal route to the Pecos Pueblo.

Later, Canyon Road served as a route for firewood-laden burros arriving from the surrounding hills to their destination on the Santa Fe plaza. Presently, this former footpath is the center of the city's art colony.

William Auclair, owner of Night Sky Gallery at 826 Canyon Road, presented me with this unusual account of his family's experience with a "past occupant."

William Auclair's Story

In 1986, I bought this house from an obstetrician, Dr. Moskowitz. My wife and I intended to remodel the interior of the house and use the front portion, facing the street, as an art gallery, maintaining the rear for our private residence. Prior to our purchase, the house had been occupied by renters for close to five years, but before he rented it out, the doctor had lived in the rear of the house and used a large front bedroom as a birthing room.

Two years after we had completed our remodeling efforts, Dr. Moskowitz paid us a visit. During our conversation regarding the usual social matters, the doctor casually remarked, "Have you had any unusual experiences... heard anything unusual in the house?"

I said, "Like what? I'm not sure what you mean."

Then he explained that the renters had complained from time to time that they heard human voices and unusual, unexplained sounds in some of the rooms. When I questioned him further, he admitted that the renters had insisted the house was haunted.

This got me thinking that the doctor could possibly explain some of the strange sounds my wife and I heard, so I told him about the "voice." Often we had heard the sound of a woman's voice speaking Spanish, mixed with broken English, coming from the old birthing room. Just before we hear the voice, our dog Neema begins growling and walks nervously towards the door of the room. Neema never barks, just continues growling, making a heavy, rumbling sound. Then, minutes later, we hear the woman's voice. This usually happened between three and four in the morning.

William Auclair

It always wakes us up, and either my wife or I open the door and peer into the empty, darkened room. Immediately, the voice stops, and for the remainder of the night, remains silenced. We've noticed that we hear the voice only during the winter months and that the spirit never seems contentious or malicious. In fact, the voice is quite soothing. . . rather gentle, calm. I imagine the spirit only wants to make her presence known.

The doctor was not very helpful regarding our "voice," but I did learn something further about it from a visitor. One day, an older, Hispanic gentleman came in, and we began a polite conversation. Then he told me he had once been a resident of our gallery-home and that his great-grandmother had died in the very room from which we heard the gentle voice. I decided not to tell him about our experience yet, and he continued. He said that after his great-grandmother had died, he and his brothers and sisters didn't want to sleep in her room because they could see her spirit materialize and try to talk to them. Being children, they pulled the blankets up over their heads and yelled for their parents.

At this point I stopped him and told him about our "voice." He did not seem surprised, but at that moment, we were interrupted by some visitors asking about a piece of framed art. He bid me farewell, and I have not seen him since that day.

I'm convinced that things are not always as they seem... that when a person dies, that is not necessarily the end of their spirit. There are moments when I feel the close presence of someone in the room with me. Even though I bought and hold title to this building, I know that I do not own it. I believe that the original owner still holds a spiritual claim on it and my family and I are simply its current caretakers.

Night Sky Gallery, Canyon Road

The Legal Tender

Constructed in 1881, the Legal Tender was originally known as The Annex Saloon and much later, in the mid 1950's, it was called the Pink Garter Saloon. Over the years it has enjoyed a reputation as a dance hall, vaudeville theatre, general store, and fine restaurant.

Various owners contributed much to modifying the building, adding priceless art work, Victorian era furnishings, and the hand-carved, cherrywood bar imported from Germany in 1894. It was renamed The Legal Tender in 1969, and the American Room, with its distinctive tinned ceiling, train station windows, and antique decorations, was added.

Throughout the years, ghosts have been observed nonchalantly meandering among the guests. The apparitions include the "Man in Black," reputed to have picked up a stray bullet during a gambling dispute, the "Lady in White," who wears an elegant, white Victorian gown, and a child in a long dress. The stories of the woman and the child are unknown, but the "Lady in White" has been seen gliding up the steps toward the balcony, and the child was observed sitting on the steps.

Emma Cordova's Story

I have worked at the Legal Tender restaurant for nearly fifteen years and have experienced several encounters with what I call ghosts. I saw the ghosts when Mr. Anderson was the owner. One night, after a busy day of waiting tables, I was helping Bertha, the bartender, clean up the bar area. As I finished wiping off a table, a strange feeling came over me, causing me to pause and look at the front door. At that moment, I noticed Bertha—staring in the same direction. Simultaneously, we saw the same unexplainable sight.

A short man, a stranger, drifted in from the outside and nonchalantly passed between us, making his way around the bar counter to the soda and water dispensers. He took a clean glass, drew himself a Coca-Cola, and drank it. Then he placed the empty glass on the bar and walked past us into the dining room where he disappeared, simply evaporated into the air.

Although Bertha and I were baffled and shaken by the experience, we managed to observe some important details. The man was dressed in the style of a by-gone era, wearing a top hat and black suit. However, he had no face! The area where his face should have been was a blur. He was not wearing a bandanna or any theatrical device; the face area was simply devoid of flesh, as if someone had taken an eraser and rubbed out his nose, mouth and eyes.

Bertha and I decided not to share this experience with anyone for fear we'd be accused of drinking on the job—or worse.

Throughout the years, I have seen this scenario played out three times, but each of these times I was alone. The man entered, took his drink, then disappeared into the atmosphere of the dining room. He never addressed me.

On two other occasions, I saw a different ghostly figure. One day, as I was working with several other employees in one of the smaller dining areas in the "Parlor Room," I suddenly caught the scent of a flowery perfume. We all smelled it, and I soon learned that this scent heralded the appearance of the "woman in white."

Emma Cordova

Later, when I was alone in the bar, I turned toward the stairs to the balcony, and there I saw a woman, about 5'5" tall, standing on the fourth step. She stared at me for less than a minute then turned and leisurely ascended the stairs. At the top, she disappeared, slowly. As with the faceless man, the woman, with waist-length black hair and long-sleeved white gown, never said a word.

I have experienced one other unexplainable occurrence. One morning, about a week after one of my encounters with the faceless man, my husband and I arrived at the restaurant to do some general cleaning up. As I was mopping on the first floor, my husband, who had gone upstairs, called out, "Emma, come here quick!" I dropped the mop and raced up the short flight of stairs. I found my husband standing beside a small round table. On the table was a dinner plate with a freshly cooked, New York steak and a baked potato with melting butter, sour cream and chives. Steam was still rising from the food. A glass of red wine and a glass of water stood like sentinels beside the plate.

We decided that somehow an intruder had entered and cooked himself a nice meal, so we dashed to the kitchen. As soon as I entered the room, I knew it had not been used recently—the grill and the oven were stone cold and clean. I got goose bumps and a chill ran down my spine. We never learned where the food had come from or who had cooked it.

These experiences puzzled and frightened me. Although I'm no longer afraid, I do feel a chilling sensation whenever I recall them.

Raymond Taylor's Stories

I am Raymond Taylor, the current owner of the Legal Tender restaurant in Lamy, New Mexico. I have owned the restaurant for over seven years, and although I have not personally witnessed ghosts or spirits, I have sound reasons to believe they exist and inhabit this building. Perhaps they are waiting for the appropriate moment to appear to me—as they have done to patrons and some of my employees.

I recall the experience of one former employee, Joe, a dishwasher and janitor, that happened in the winter of 1987. One evening at about seven, I began my daily task of closing out the bar cash register. Everyone except for Joe and me had gone home. We were the only "living" beings in the entire building.

The Legal Tender Co-Owners, Amy Cort and Raymond Taylor.

Joe, who was about fifty years old at the time, was working at the opposite end of the restaurant in the hall area between the kitchen and the storage section.

As I was working, I suddenly heard the sound of approaching footsteps. I turned to see Joe, mop and bucket in hand, coming towards me. He was pale and unusually jittery.

Haltingly, he asked, "How long have you been in the bar?"

I replied, "About five minutes, why?"

He said, "Oh, nothing," and returned to the kitchen. He quickly finished cleaning up and immediately went home.

Joe worked three more nights then quit.

It wasn't until about a week later that I learned of Joe's strange experience. I was talking to a few other employees and found out that that night, as Joe was mopping the hall floor, he felt a shove, as if someone had pushed him out of their way. He assumed it was me and never looked up. But, when he came into the bar and saw me busy at the cash register, he realized I could not have pushed him. Since we were the only people in the building, Joe concluded that a spirit had made contact with him.

Babe, my general manager, told me of another spiritual encounter. One night, while replacing a roll of paper towels in the men's bathroom, he glanced to the side of the room and saw the disembodied head of a woman materialize. He said that the apparition hovered, suspended in the air for about fifteen seconds, then slowly disappeared as he stared at it.

I learned of another ghostly meeting when I met and conversed with two regular patrons from the nearby El Dorado community. They told me that they continually chose to sit in a specific section of the dining room because they hoped to see the spirits again. I asked for an explanation.

Apparently, one Sunday evening, as they were having dinner, the woman excused herself to visit the ladies' room. When she returned, she told her husband about the extraordinary couple she had seen as she was coming back to their table. The woman was dressed in long-sleeved white dress and had long dark hair, hanging loosely down her back. She was accompanied by a Hispanic man with a moustache who wore a dark suit. Because of their unusual dress and stately appearances, the woman who had observed them decided to take a closer look. So as she passed the curious couple, she turned her head in their direction. They were gone. They had disappeared in the time it takes to blink an eye.

Casa Real

There are presently three senior health care centers in the city of Santa Fe. Built in 1985, Casa Real, at 501 Galisteo Street, is a 112 bed convalescent center.

As most of the older city residents can attest, the land on which Casa Real stands was originally the location of the state of New Mexico's penitentiary graveyard. Various criminals and "outlaws" of the old west were incarcerated at the penitentiary. Murderers were executed by hanging, and because they were usually denied burial in consecrated cemeteries, they were buried at the penitentiary graveyard.

David Rodriguez's Story

Since the day I began my employment at Casa Real, I was ill at ease and uncomfortable whenever I was inside the building. I felt a strange atmosphere of uneasiness about the place—like there was a heavy pressure on my shoulders or a pair of invisible eyes watching my every move.

Nurses, nurses aides, patients, visitors and office staff all have stories to tell about this place. Most of the stories and personal experiences regarding Casa Real have occurred during the night—probably because of the quiet, eerie silence. Some of the nurses have approached me concerning strange, unexplainable loud clapping noises; at other times, people reported hearing the moans of a person in great pain coming from an empty room. I've come to regard these numerous experiences of the medical staff as a clear indication that something very strange is going on in this place.

One morning, two night nurses were visibly shaken as they recounted to me their experience of the night before. They said that while walking the corridor between the north and south side of the facility, one of the nurses, Nurse Newport, decided to pay her respects to a deceased patient she had known. The coroner had been called minutes earlier to remove the body. As she entered the room, nothing seemed out of the ordinary: the windows were closed and the curtains drawn. But as she viewed the lifeless body on the bed, suddenly a crisp, chilling air enveloped her. Although the doors and windows were shut tight, the rosary pinned to the wall above the bed swung from side to side as if moving on its own power. Somewhat hysterical, Nurse Newport ran to the nurse's station, where a fellow nurse tried to calm her down.

When the coroner arrived, the other nurse, Nurse Parra, packed the deceased patient's few personal articles into a cardboard box for the family. But about two hours later, after the room had been emptied, the nurse call light above the door went on. The nurse who had cleaned the room went to investigate, found nothing and reset the call button. About thirty minutes later, the light came on again. Thinking there might be a short in the wiring, the nurse returned to the empty room, unplugged the call button and cord, and placed them on the freshly made bed for the maintenance personnel.

Not more than ten minutes later, the light above the deceased patient's room came on again. This time, both nurses were very shaken, so several minutes later, they went together to the room to unscrew the light bulb. While one nurse was up on a chair, Nurse Newport suddenly turned and ran to the nurses' station, yelling as she went "Something grabbed me!"

Before the nurse on the chair could react, she felt a blanket of chilling air envelop her legs. She jumped down and immediately returned to the station where both nurses remained all night.

Two years ago, we admitted an elderly Native American woman from a nearby pueblo. As she was wheeled into the lobby, she asked her family to pause. She looked around, and with the sound of discomfort in her voice, announced that there were "bad spirits in this place." She resolved to get out as soon as possible, and a few days later, she was transferred to another facility.

These experiences are not isolated. For a long time incidents of moaning, strange noises and other phenomena have been taking place regularly in empty rooms of the north and south wings. However, all this would soon end. Recently one of our patients had a Native American visitor. This woman visitor asked to speak with the administrator about something very important, so I met with her. She informed me that she felt a "distinctive atmosphere of unearthly beings seized and held within the walls of Casa Real."

"You have a lot of spirits in here," she stated. "I will take care of them if you want."

I told her that I was interested in her assessment and would like to hear more about how she would rid the building of its "spirits." She then said that she would return in a few days with the materials she needed and perform the ritual.

Although I was unsure of what to expect, I agreed and in the rush of daily work, soon forgot about our brief meeting.

Four days later, the woman returned and met me in my office—ready to perform the ritual. She said that I would have to be still and speak only when she gave me the signal. I nodded my head in agreement. Then she brought out small bundles of herbs from her purse and a leather pouch which she called her "medicine bag."

She burned the herb bundles in an ash tray and after reciting a prayer and petitions, drew from her bag a collection of small stones of various colors and shapes. Again she chanted a prayer and burned more herbs.

Next she gave me a candle, a book of matches and a copper ring. She instructed me to burn the candle and to set the copper ring over and around the lit candle. After I did this, she blew out the candle and presented me with both the candle and the copper ring. She told me to light the candle again at the next full moon and allow it to burn itself out. Then, at the following full moon, I was to take the copper ring and bury it in the inner courtyard of the facility. I thanked her, and she left.

For days I kept both the candle and the copper ring in my desk, occasionally glancing at them. When the full moon arrived, I did as the woman had requested. I felt it couldn't hurt. So with the assistant director of nurses at my side, I lit the candle and let it burn itself out. For the following full moon, we located a suitable place and buried the copper ring in the courtyard garden. As of that date neither my staff nor I have experienced any strange or ghostly phenomena. I hope that whatever is buried deep within the foundations of this building stays quiet and at peace—at least until the day I move on.

David Rodriguez, Casa Real Administrator.

The Lady in Room 222

Although it was a year ago, it is still very difficult for me to think about the experience I had at Casa Real. I do not want to experience anything like that again. Try as I may, I have not been able to erase it from my mind, and I definitely believe there is reason to wonder about the existence of life after death.

When I was the facility director of nurses at Casa Real, I was responsible for supervising the nurses, making sure the patients were on their proper medications and ensuring that doctors' orders were being followed. Due to a shortage of nurses, I often worked the night shift to make sure the facility was properly staffed.

Three days prior to the night of my experience, an elderly woman with terminal cancer was admitted. Although in much pain, the woman, was lucid, aware of her surroundings and had a clear understanding of her prognosis. When dealing with the staff, she attempted to disguise the inevitability of her death. We soon learned that this lady had been active and socially involved in the business of living before her illness befell her.

The only time she complained was when we had to change her bed linen. The nurse's aides had to gather around her bed and turn or lift her while the sheets were changed. In her dear, sweet manner, she always apologized for her short moans of discomfort.

On the third day of her stay, the woman abruptly refused to take food. When I arrived later that evening, I immediately learned of her grave condition. A few hours before I had come on duty, she had regressed to a comatose state. The woman was now placed on close observation and I.V. therapy in order to keep her hydrated. But our efforts were in vain, and a few hours later she lapsed into a deep coma with no response to outside stimuli. From my many years of experience, I knew that once a terminal cancer patient reaches this stage, death soon follows.

I remember the details of that night vividly and completely. I recall specifically the manner in which her hair was combed, the pattern of her nightgown and especially her hands—marked with dark blue and purple blotches from the numerous needle pricks.

Not long after she passed away, the paramedics from St. Vincent Hospital arrived, and I was called on the intercom. I proceeded from my office towards her room, number 222, but I stopped at the end of the hall and watched the paramedics take her draped body out of the room on a stretcher. I just stood there and watched, not wanting to interfere with the process.

As soon as they left her room and turned into the hallway, I noticed the nurse call light above the door to her room came on. There was no reason for the staff to turn the light on in an empty room. I thought in their haste, the paramedics might have dropped the call button on the floor, triggering the light. I waited for someone to reset the button. Strangely enough, no one did.

But stranger still was what happened next. As the stretcher passed each patient's room, the nurse call light above the doors lit up. I could not move a muscle. I stood there, overcome with amazement and fright at the sight of the lights going on as the woman's body passed each door.

As the stretcher reached the nurses' station at the opposite end of the hall, I could watch no longer. I felt the hair on the back of my neck stand on end. I yelled to the paramedics to look at the lights, but they did not grasp my meaning. Their eyes were focused on the exit door ahead of them.

Such a great fear came over me—I think I became hysterical because I rushed out of the building into the parking lot. There I gathered my senses, took a deep breath and watched the ambulance drive away into the darkness. Then I looked up at the moon and stars. I knew I had just had an experience in the dimension of the dead.

La Posada Hotel

Two centuries before the first voyage of Columbus, Indians cultivated the alluvial terraces of the Santa Fe River. The ground on which La Posada now is situated had a fresh water spring and, with its location near the river, was undoubtedly farmed by the residents of surrounding pueblos.

After the Spaniards arrived in 1610, the land remained under cultivation serving the area as prime agricultural land for the new Spanish inhabitants.

An irrigation ditch (the Acequia de La Loma) was constructed along the course of what is now Palace Avenue. This acequia was joined by the Acequia de la Guardia, producing a water system which bisected this land, and was fed in part by the spring providing the principal source of water to the area.

In the Pueblo revolt, the Indians cut off the acequias, forcing the evacuation of the Spaniards. Later, Don Diego DeVargas, who is credited with the bloodless conquest of the Pueblo Indians of the area, cut off the acequias to drive the Indians out when he reclaimed Santa Fe.

Julie Staab's Room

While the precise date of acquisition is unknown, by the early 19th century the La Posada property was owned by the Baca family. This family is one of Santa Fe's oldest, having been one of the four original settlers that returned to Santa Fe from El Paso del Norte after expulsion of the Indians by DeVargas.

By the 1850's, Palace Avenue had developed as a public street, and in the succeeding fifty years it was to become the fashionable residential district in Santa Fe.

Portions of the Baca property bordering Palace Avenue and lying east of the present entry way to La Posada were conveyed after 1850 to Doña Francisca Hinojas. The widow of a member of another pioneer Santa Fe family (arriving shortly after 1700), Doña Hinojas was related to the Baca family. Some of her acquisitions were by inheritance from the Bacas and some were by purchase. Doña Hinojas constructed a fine residence at 355 Palace Avenue which still exists. Other portions of her property were subdivided and resold.

In 1876 one of these parcels was acquired by Abraham Staab,

who, with three of his older brothers, had emigrated to Santa Fe from Germany, in the mid 1800's. They established one of the major mercantile businesses in the burgeoning capital and rose to civic importance. Along with other prominent Jewish families, they maintained a close relationship with Archbishop Lamy, and were major contributors to the building fund of the new St. Francis Cathedral.

Now prosperous, Abraham went back to Germany to find a bride. He married Julie Schuster and brought her to a modest adobe house on Burro Alley. There she bore four boys and four girls—raising seven to adulthood. The death of an infant son turned Julie's hair prematurely white. Because of her frequent pregnancies and what an early diary calls only a "dreadful accident," Julie Staab was an invalid most of her life, suffering from bouts of severe depression and illness.

In 1884, as he'd promised his bride years before, Abraham Staab commissioned the building of a three-story brick house on Palace Avenue. Here the Staabs entertained lavishly. Julie was a gracious hostess, health permitting. Visitors from the East, members of old Spanish families, military officers and special friends like Archbishop Lamy and the Lew Wallaces all attended these social events.

Abraham Staab ruled with an iron hand, controlling his children's destinies for decades. When son Arthur married a gentile woman, Abraham disinherited him. Teddy, a doctor in the East, was called home so often for his mother's illnesses that he eventually gave up his practice. Daughter Bertha became engaged three times to upstanding young men of good families, but Abraham always objected. Later he tried to force her to marry a man she and everyone else disliked. She was 35 before she won his approval to marry a man of her own choosing.

Although of different faith, Abraham loaned considerable sums to help construct St. Francis Cathedral. When the mortgages came due, Archbishop Lamy announced sadly that the church could not repay. Abraham forgave the debt, and in gratitude, the Archbishop directed that the Hebrew inscription "Jehovah" be placed over the cathedral doors.

Abraham Staab was one of the founders and first presidents of the Santa Fe Chamber of Commerce and a director of the First

National Bank. He helped persuade officials of the Denver and Rio Grande Railroad to establish a branch from Santa Fe to Chama, and he was largely responsible for keeping the State Capitol in Santa Fe.

Julie Staab died in 1896 at age 52, in her bedroom. Her troubled spirit is believed by many to still roam the upper floor of the Staabs' former home. Abraham died in 1913, and shortly thereafter, the third floor of the family home burned. The residence was later restored and converted to an inn, with cottages where the large orchard and gardens had been.

The role of the Staabs and the Staab Mansion in Santa Fe life of the late nineteenth century has been noted by local historians:

"The social life of New Mexico's capitol, the brilliant functions of frequent occurrence given by the ladies and officers of old Fort Marcy... are wondrous memories with those who were privileged to participate. In those social sidelights of Santa Fe history, the Staab Mansion on Palace Avenue played prominently. Magnificent in their simplicity were the contributions of Abraham and Mrs. Staab, with their older daughters... Attended by dignitaries, military and civilian, governors, justices, visiting notables, and officers of high rank, these entertainments made life at Fort Marcy and Old Santa Fe preferable to that in many of the great regimental posts of the far west."[1]

---

1   Ralph Twitchel, *Old Santa Fe* (1925) Quoted by Floyd S. Fierman, "The Staabs of Santa Fe" *Rio Grande History* (1983)

Shortly after the turn of the century, the third story of the Staab Mansion containing the ballroom, was destroyed in a fire. It was never rebuilt and the residence ceased to have the distinctive mansard roof seen in early drawings and photographs. Other major Santa Fe buildings in the Second Empire Style have met similar or worse fates.

At about the same time as the Staab Mansion was constructed, a brick residence was built by Ramon Baca at the corner of Palace Avenue and Paseo de Peralta. This residence incorporated portions of adobe structures which dated to the 17th century. Even after the residence was constructed, Baca continued to farm the bulk of what is now La Posada.

In 1934 the Baca holdings were acquired by R.H. and Eulalia Nason. Originally from Kansas City and Chicago, Nason had moved to Santa Fe for his health. In 1936 the Nasons acquired the old Staab property from the First National Bank of Santa Fe after its acquisition by foreclosure.

Strongly immersed in the Pueblo Revival movement, Nason constructed a series of casitas in the ancient manner, building adobes on the site from local clay and straw without plans or formal design.

The Second Empire and Victorian features of the Staab era were de-emphasized and gradually subsumed as a Pueblo-style inn was created on the site. The Nasons called it "La Posada" meaning inn or lodging or resting place in Spanish.

Florencita's Story

The following is a story told to be by Florecita Solis, a longtime resident of Santa Fe. Florecita's story is no doubt a difficult one to imagine for the average reader, however with a little understanding of the human desire for maliciousness, maybe not so difficult.

My experience with the supernatural happened when I was only fourteen years of age. Although many traumatic things happen to children, my personal experience with evil left me with no doubt that I will carry the after-effects of my encounter throughout my adult life.

It began innocently enough one warm afternoon when my brothers and I decided to follow the Santa Fe riverbank from our neighborhood as it made its way through the landscape southward. We wanted to see how far we could travel. It was my idea, but my brothers were elated.

"Sure, we might even find some gold or something," said my brother Vicente.

My brother Fidel located a large tree that had been struck by lightening, and we broke off branches to make walking sticks. Then with Oso, our dog, we set off on our "big adventure."

After following the river's winding curves and valleys for over two hours, we came upon a thicket of cottonwood trees.

When I joined my brothers, who had gathered on the river bank, I saw a structure on the other side of the river. We decided to investigate. We crossed the river at its narrowest point, using large rock boulders that had been lodged in the debris as stepping stones.

Once on the other side, I saw that the structure was an old abandoned adobe house. Its earthen walls lay in a large crumbling rubble on the ground, but the half-collapsed chimney and part of the roof were still intact. So we climbed onto the roof and threw pebbles towards the river.

My brother Gregorio said, "I think I know whose house this

is. It was the witch's, Diego Blanco, *'El Zorrillo.'* Remember the story about him?"

We all knew the story because my father and his friends inevitably brought up the subject whenever they gathered together for a late night song and drink.

El Zorrillo

Diego Blanco was a man in his late fifties who had built his home on the outskirts of the city soon after he arrived from the eastern part of the state. He told the few people he chose to talk to that he was from the Mora valley area.

He was tall and had a large streak of light grey hair that started on the left side of his forehead and ended behind his left ear. My father always referred to him as *El Zorrillo*, the skunk. Because his reputation as a practitioner of witchcraft was well known throughout Santa Fe, he was not welcomed in the city. So he settled further down the river.

Soon after *El Zorrillo's* arrival, he befriended a young Indian, Eliseo, from the Tesuque pueblo, who helped him build his home. Several months later, when Eliseo did not show up for the pueblo corn dance ceremony, the other members of the pueblo decided something had happened to him.

The pueblo members were very concerned, and many people, both Spanish and Indian, rode out on horseback to search the surrounding mountains. They found nothing... no evidence of what had become of Eliseo.

Then, one morning, many months later, a woman and her two grandchildren climbed to the top of a small mesa near the pueblo looking for herbs. There they found Eliseo's partially decomposed body. My father told us that the body had been painted with some sort of black paint and his hair was covered in an offensive smelling sap or juice that had hardened. Because the body was missing two fingers on each hand, the pueblo people claimed that Eliseo had been tortured and killed in devotion to the devil. Everyone immediately assumed that *El Zorrillo* was responsible for the gruesome deed.

Because my father traded with the Tesuque natives, they asked him to join them in confronting *El Zorrillo*. On horseback, the men followed the river for several miles, eventually coming upon the grove of cottonwoods and the house. Dressed only in trousers, *El Zorrillo* came to the door and yelled every known obscenity at them.

He looked straight into the eyes of one of Eliseo's uncles and shouted in Spanish, "Sons of the great demon, remove your rotted bodies and filthy animals from my property!"

As he screamed, his face became twisted with rage and large

globs of foam appeared at the corners of his beastly mouth. He was so overwhelmed with anger that his words became muffled and indistinguishable. At one point he began spitting at the men in an animal-like manner. Then he moved to the outside wall of his house and began slapping his hands against the wall, calling out the names of Lucifer, Satan and other dark angels of hell.

When one of Eliseo's uncles picked up a dead branch and threw it at *El Zorrillo*, the men gathered their courage and made a dash towards the madman, overpowering him. As they wrestled with him and got a good whiff of his body, the men learned why he was called the skunk. My father had worked in a pork processing plant, so he immediately recognized the putrid odor of rotted pig blood and urine.

They managed to bind him securely, and then the men entered the house. In spite of the dimness inside (the windows were covered with gunnysacks), my father found, hanging on the south wall, a wooden crucifix about four feet by four feet painted black and red, with a human finger nailed to each end of the cross—Eliseo's missing fingers. The putrid smell of the house became so offensive that the men finally had to run outside. Then they discovered that *El Zorrillo* had escaped—rope and all. The next morning about twenty or thirty people from the pueblo went to the house and burned it, reciting prayers to disburse the evil *El Zorrillo* had brought with him. That was the last anyone ever saw or heard of *El Zorrillo*.

Because we knew the story so well, my brothers and I were convinced that we had stumbled upon the ruins of Diego Blanco's home, but the bright sunlight of the afternoon and the cooing of the desert doves made it seem like just another old adobe ruin. We felt unthreatened by its evil history and began rummaging among the rubble. Pushing aside burnt boards and twisted metal, we occasionally disturbed a lizard. Fidel found an old shoe and threw it at me, bopping me on the head. I remember him saying that the old shoe belonged to *El Zorrillo* and it would follow me home. Then my younger brother yelled that he had found something.

We joined him at a mound of broken blue glass, and he pointed with his walking stick at a small black book. As we examined it, we saw that most of the pages were burned and covered in red mud. About 20 pages, written in long hand, remained intact. Fidel wiped off the mud and examined it carefully. He told us it contained instructions on witchcraft. We took his word for it and swore not to tell our parents. Fidel took charge of the book and said he would take it to the church and sprinkle holy water on it. With grave authority, he told us that the holy water would conquer any evil left in it. We voiced our approval and promised not to tell anyone—not even our friends.

I whistled for Oso and we began our trek home. On the return trip, Fidel stopped and read some of the pages to himself. He told us they were instructions for summoning a spirit. My younger brother asked him to stop reading because the sun was beginning to set and he was getting scared. Fidel put the book away and we proceeded home.

The next day, Fidel told me he had taken the book to the Saint Francis Cathedral, sprinkled holy water on it and placed it behind the altar. Later, I learned that he and my younger brother Vicente had taken the book behind some haystacks and read it

in secret. Fidel had never gone to the cathedral. But I did not find this out until one terrifying night about a week after we had found the book.

My parents had to go to a wake in the small town of Chamita, north of Santa Fe, and left us in charge of our baby sister. That night, Fidel brought out the book and told us he would entertain us by reading it. At first I was angry, but my curiosity got the better of me.

Fidel read a passage. It instructed that there be two windows at opposite ends of the room. Since the room we had gathered in had the windows, we decided to follow the instructions. We opened the windows, and Fidel read aloud some strange prayers and the names of archaic angels. Next, my brother Daniel wrote the foreign symbols in salt on the floor. Then we just sat there and waited. When nothing happened, we laughed nervously and joked about the mess on the floor.

As I reached for a kerosene lamp on the table so I could go to the kitchen to give Oso the soup bones my mother had left for him, I heard a strange noise outside. I froze. Oso was barking and growling and scratching wildly at the back door. The sound like a low cracking of thunder continued, but it was a clear, star-filled night without a cloud in the sky. Then a strong wind billowed the curtains, and everything in the room shook. Suddenly we heard the sound of a man screaming, and the cracking noise got louder.

We were so frightened that we ran under the table. The curtains swayed wildly from side to side, rose to the ceiling and fell. Oso had stopped barking and scratching, but the chilling screams increased, ending in mad laughter. We cried and prayed at the same time. My bother held my baby sister close as we covered our faces with our arms. The screams continued, increasing in intensity. It was awful.

The kerosene lamps flew off the tables and dashed onto the floor. Kerosene oil spilled everywhere; we were bathed in it. But somehow the house did not catch on fire. I peeked over my arms and caught the image of a large shadow of a human being standing in the middle of the room.

I yelled, "It's the devil!"

The image had very long hair flying all around its head, but in the darkness, I could not make out the facial features. Then this evil-looking figure raised its left hand up over its head and threw its head back, letting out the most awful scream I had ever heard...or could imagine. We were all crying loudly and uncontrollably as another blood-curdling scream came from this thing. The windows shattered and slivers of glass flew in all directions.

Suddenly, everything stopped. The wind, the screams-everything came to a complete halt. We were praying the Our Father, the Hail Mary and any prayer we could make up. Our arms and faces were covered with dirt, tears, and glittering shards of glass. But the stress of the experience had taken its toll, and we soon fell asleep.

I'm not sure how much time elapsed before the sound of our parents' footsteps and voices awakened us. We ran to the door shouting and talking at once. After seeing our tear-stained faces, my mother cried in distress and shook me, asking what had happened.

We regained our composure and described the book, the ritual and the demon spirit that we had conjured up from hell. My parents could not hide their shock as they entered the house and saw its condition. The strong scent of sulfur overpowered the smell of kerosene.

Then my father lit a lamp and held it up, and we clearly saw the damage. The curtains that my mother had laboriously sewn hung in shreds, and strips of curtain fabric littered the floor. But, most frightening of all, were the large claw marks etched deeply into the walls. It appeared as if a large, cat-like animal had savagely dragged its claws across the walls. Even pieces of glass left in the windows had vicious scratches on them.

That night we all stayed at my uncle Raphael's small, two bedroom adobe. We were cramped but safe. It was difficult to erase from our minds the image we had seen earlier, and the stench of sulfur lingered on our clothes. My father lit a candle and placed a small *santo* (statue of a saint) of the *Virgen de Dolores* by our bedside. Eventually we were lulled to sleep by our parents' soft voices as they prayed the rosary. I vividly remember the closeness of the family and the yellow glow of the bouncing candle light in the small room.

The following morning, accompanied by relatives and neighbors, we returned to our home. A priest came along to bless the house and remove the remains of the book. We searched every corner of the house but never found the book. My mother opened the back door then rushed back in, crying that the devil had killed our dog.

Slumped against the side of the house, with an expression of terror frozen on its face, was Oso's lifeless body. His mouth was partially open, exposing the teeth on one side of his face. He looked as if he had been growling. The strangest thing about Oso's body was that when he was alive, he had a beautiful reddish brown coat, but now, after his brush with terror, his entire coat had turned a light grey.

As I reached out to stroke my dog, my father held me back and said, "It is better for you not to touch him. He suffered a lot, and we cannot be sure that the evil influence is not still on him."

We all cried for our dog.

Later that same day, my uncles built a large bonfire and tossed into the flames every bit of evidence that remained from our experience...including the lifeless body of my dog.

Now, as an adult woman, I think back to that time and sadly reflect on the faces gathered around the fire. I will never forget that night as long as I live. Never.

Ten Thousand Waves

Located three and a half miles from downtown Santa Fe, Ten Thousand Waves is a health spa with hot tubs, modeled after the hot springs resorts of Japan. The following story, related to me by the owner, Duke Klauch, gives much food for thought.

Duke's Story

Six years ago I bought this property. At that time, it was elevated land covered in piñon and juniper trees, and it included a house and horse corral. Because of its isolation and raw beauty, this piece of land would be the perfect setting for Ten Thousand Waves. The main road was the only trace of civilization in this verdant, mountain spot.

I purchased the property from Elizabeth Zinn, who had inherited it from her mother, also named Elizabeth. The mother had constructed the house before the birth of her daughter, and few improvements had been made since it was built. When the daughter grew up, she married and moved away.

Gradually, the elder Elizabeth became ill. She died and was buried somewhere on the mountain. Upon the death of her mother, Elizabeth returned and lived in the house her mother had built.

Once I purchased the land and buildings and signed all the paperwork, I moved into the house and tried to make it "my home." I focused on landscaping and interior decoration. The years of neglect had taken their toll.

However, not long after I moved into the house, I experienced what I call "ghostly events." There were nights when I was awakened by what sounded like iron hitting iron or chains and metal items being dragged across the hardwood floors. I'd sit up in bed, peer into the darkness, and listen. Eventually, I would get out of bed and walk around the house, searching for a clue to the origin of the noises. After making the rounds in the murky darkness, I would return to bed, having discovered nothing unusual. I did notice that at the times the sounds awakened me, the clock face on top of my dresser marked 3:00 a.m.

Once, a woman friend of mine spent several nights at the house. She slept at the opposite end, and one morning she told me of her frightening experience. She said that during the night, she had been awakened from her sleep by unidentified noises. Then, she noticed faint movements in the dark room and immediately felt a strong, heavy pressure on her chest. This pressure was so powerful that she was unable to move. It felt as if her whole body was wrapped in a tight cloth. Unable to move even one finger, she remained in this condition for what seemed like two hours. She was, in her own words, "totally terrified." She described the presence as very strong and overwhelming. She believed it was a man. Needless to say, thereafter she spent her nights at her own home.

One evening, Ms Zinn, the previous owner, and her husband came over for dinner, and I soon learned some very unsettling details about the history of my property.

Toward the end of dinner, Elizabeth, unaware of my experiences, asked, "Have you seen my daughter?"

"I don't know your daughter," I said.

"She's dead," responded Ms Zinn.

I was taken back by her comments. But before I could respond, Ms Zinn told me the following.

Her daughter Evelyn was having a party with some friends late one night at the house. The daughter was distraught about something, and at about 3 A.M. in the evening, took a hand gun from her father's dresser drawer, walked to the horse corral, placed the barrel to her head and pulled the trigger.

Less than a year later, in utter despair over his daughter's suicide, Ms Zinn's first husband looped a rope over one of the *vigas* (beams) in the living room and hanged himself.

Several years before I bought the property, Ms Zinn had rented it to a local physician. One night, as the doctor was strolling by the horse corral (now the lower parking lot), he heard someone call his name. He turned and saw a young girl in a long white dress. He called out sharply, "What are you doing on this property?" She did not respond, and as he stared at her, she slowly disappeared before his eyes.

Needless to say, for the remainder of that evening I was very uncomfortable, and once the Zinns left, I decided to put the whole story out of my head and get on with my life. At first, it appeared that I was going to be successful.

I began work on the major project of building Ten Thousand Waves. During the construction, it was necessary to blast and level large portions of the upper hillside to accommodate the various buildings and the road that presently runs from the highway to the upper level parking lot. Although there are no records describing the exact location of the elder Elizabeth's interment, I now suspect that the construction crew may have destroyed, moved, or upset the grave in some way. I do know that Ms Zinn's mother died over sixty years ago. However, I had lost touch with the Zinn family and had no way of establishing the location of the burial site.

When I opened the business in 1981, "ghostly events" began to occur almost immediately. A fellow by the name of Ted was in charge of opening the business each morning at 7:00 a.m. He told me more than once that while he was alone in the dressing rooms, making sure everything was in order, he had heard footsteps on the stairs—coming up from the main entrance, proceeding along the halls, and arriving at his location. But as the footfalls arrived, Ted could see nothing, so he would go to the front lobby and check the main doors. Invariably they were locked with the dead bolt firmly set.

This series of events happened to Ted almost daily. But soon things progressed. He would hear the main doors open and close with a loud slam, but after investigation, he found nothing. Then, one morning, Ted felt a presence in the room with him. He says that as he turned, he caught sight of the misty, white figure of a woman, standing absolutely still. Then, as he watched the figure slowly disappeared.

At this point, Ted and I decided we were dealing with something weird and that we'd better do something about it. Ted contacted a priest at the St. Francis Cathedral in town about the possibility of conducting an exorcism. After Ted told our story, the priest said he would see what he could do. A few days later, a car pulled up and three priests got out. I showed them to an office area where they changed into the habits of the Franciscan order. They had brought incensors, holy water, a crucifix, and a Bible.

Proceeding throughout the establishment, the three read passages from the Bible and sprinkled holy water. From hot tub to hot tub, dressing rooms to the grounds—the three holy men made their rounds. When they had completed this procedure of cleansing, they approached the front lobby and placed a small wooden crucifix next to the Japanese bell on the wall behind the main counter. The crucifix remains there to this day.

Since the visit of the priests, I have not heard or seen any ghostly activities—except for once. One night while dusting, a cleaning lady removed the crucifix and placed it on the counter next to the cash register. After she finished dusting, she forgot to replace the cross, and no one noticed it had been moved.

Soon, members of the staff began complaining that they heard the sound of footsteps and other noises they could not explain. When word finally reached me about these incidents, I immediately questioned the staff and eventually discovered the missing crucifix. I soon found it and restored it to its original resting place, instructing my employees to make certain it was never moved again. We have had no further disturbances.

Given the suicides of the young woman and her father and the possibility that we disturbed the grandmother's grave, I am convinced that their restless spirits remain on the property. I am grateful that—at least for the moment—all is peaceful at Ten Thousand Waves.

St. Vincent Hospital

St. Vincent Hospital, Santa Fe's newest and largest, was completed in July of 1977. This three-story, Catholic hospital was founded by the Sisters of Charity. The hospital, as well as the nearby health care facility, Casa Real, were built upon the original site of the New Mexico State Penitentiary graveyard. I had the pleasure of interviewing Maryclare Henebry, R.N. who works on the third floor in the adult psychiatric unit. People generally expect hauntings to occur in old, time-worn buildings, but her story explodes that myth. When the ghosts of Santa Fe wish to make their presence known, they choose the location with no preference for age—a 300-year old, one-room adobe or a modern, 200-bed hospital.

Maryclare's Story

I have worked at St. Vincent's for several years. Presently, I work in the adult psychiatric department which has two units: one secured, the other unsecured. The secured unit has a set of

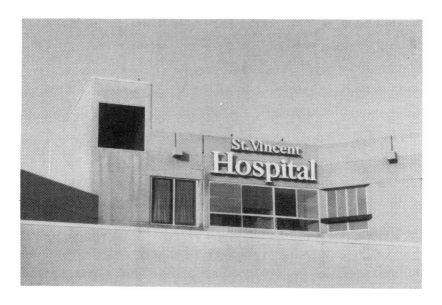

double doors which remain locked at all times because of the psychotic behavior of the patients. The doors are heavy and have a large panel of thick, shatter-proof safety glass, providing a clear, but safe, view of the hallways leading to the units.

The unsecured unit, directly across the hall, has a pair of similar doors—except they are unlocked. As the Night Charge Nurse, I frequently make visits to both units, helping with admissions and other duties.

My encounter with the supernatural occurred one night in the secured unit. At about 2:00 a.m., after I had finished my usual charting, I gathered my array of books and magazines and made my way towards the locked doors. As soon as I placed the key into the lock, I felt a presence beside me. Still holding the key, I slowly turned to my right and saw a small, Hispanic man withdrawing his hand from me, as if he had been caught attempting to touch my right shoulder.

I quickly turned away from him and moved up against the side of the door, giving me the opportunity to get a good look at him. I had assumed he was a patient who had managed to sneak by my desk, but he was somehow different. I had never seen him before, and he was dressed in a style of clothing I did not recognize. He wore dark pants, crudely stitched and made of a heavy fabric. His white shirt was buttoned at the neck, and it had a wide, old-fashioned collar. He wore black leather shoes. He was very short—I am 5'3" and I towered over him.

I was startled when I realized he was from another time. I asked him who he was, but he just stood there looking at me with his dark, bright eyes. Then, to my complete amazement, he slowly disappeared—gradually and simultaneously—from both his head and his feet. I felt a coldness envelope me.

I quickly tried to gather my faculties and make my way out of the unit into the hall. My hands were shaking so badly that I fumbled with the key as I placed it in the lock. Finally, I opened the door, rushed through and relocked it. I ran to the unit across the hall and sat at my desk. I did not mention the man to my fellow workers in the next room who were discussing a patient's treatment plans. Somehow the incident seemed out of place in this medical setting.

Knowing I had to return to the secured unit in one hour, I tried to convince myself I had imagined the man and his clothes. At 4:00 a.m., somewhat self-assured, I made my way out of the unsecured unit. The hall was well-lit and seemed safe, so with keys and charts in hand, I trudged steadily forward.

I paused at the doors, waiting for something to happen. All was quiet. I searched the brightly lit hall and looked through the glass window to the secured unit. The silence was both comforting and unsettling.

As I began slipping my key into the lock, I again saw the little man at the east end of the hallway. I froze. As I watched from behind the safety of the locked doors, I lost sight of him. But my curiosity got the better of my fear, and I pressed my face against the window, trying to see him. Then I backed away from the window, and as I did, I caught sight of another figure—a woman.

She passed quickly by me down the hall. She was a bit taller than the man and wore a white gown. Because she wore a black veil or mantilla, I could not see her face. She ran past me, and I noticed her hair fell long and loose down her back. As she

Maryclare Henebry, R.N.

passed by me, I looked down at her feet. There was nothing there. The woman was floating above the floor by two or three inches. I stood absolutely still and watched her glide along the hall, turn a corner and disappear.

Before I could get over this mentally staggering episode, the small man reappeared. He came racing down the hall, passed me and disappeared in the same manner as the woman. I got the impression that he was chasing her, and I suddenly realized that this little escapade of "cat and mouse" did not include me. I was simply a witness to some ghostly game.

Reflecting now on all that happened that night, I am drawn to the thought that perhaps I could have helped the couple. When the man first appeared, he reached out to touch me. Perhaps he was making a plea for my help. Maybe he was trying to locate a lost love. Or perhaps the man confused me with the woman in white. It is also possible that the woman was in danger, or that she was trying to escape from the man. Maybe he had killed her. I'll never know the reasons for the apparitions or why I was chosen to view them, and I've never had another experience like that. Perhaps it's just as well.

La Residencia

La Residencia is a seven-year old nursing facility located at the corner of Paseo de Peralta and Palace Avenue. Prior to October 1983, the building housed the original St. Vincent Hospital which provided for the health care needs of Santa Fe and Northern New Mexico.

Many of the city's health care workers who served there believe it to be haunted. Specifically, those nurses who completed residence work at this facility for their New Mexico nursing licenses reported its unusual history. The following narratives are based on interviews with three employees of La Residencia: the Nurse Coordinator, the Charge Nurse and the Nursing Assistant.

The Nurse Coordinator's Story: Blood in the Basement

All the nurses that I now work with and have worked with in the past are very much aware of the ghosts that dwell at La Residencia, but the basement holds its own special, grisly power. I personally can attest to this. You couldn't pay me a sack of gold to walk into that basement—day or night.

When staff members ask me to accompany them to the basement, I tell them, "The day I go back into that hell is the day I turn in my resignation!"

The basement has many rooms and hallways, and it's very dark. The state museum offices, which are located in the building next to La Residencia, use one large hallway as a storage area for Native American artifacts such as stone tools, pottery and grinding stones. I imagine these items, and others stored in large,

sealed crates, have been excavated from burial sites. Considering how non-Native Americans treat living Indians, it would not surprise me if there were skeletal remains down there in cardboard boxes.

I am convinced that there are a lot of upset spirits in that basement. Other employees have reported hearing loud banging noises and voices coming from the basement at odd hours of the day and night. No one—except for new employees—ever ventures to the elevator and presses the "B" button.

In the past, the "seasoned" staff members used to initiate new employees by escorting them to the basement and leaving them there to find their way, through the dark maze of hallways, to the stairway—without the aid of a flashlight. The only available light would be the green glow from the "Exit" signs. Eventually, the initiates—pale as a ghost—would reach the upper floor, where we would welcome them.

One evening, I was selected to accompany a new nurse's aide to the basement for this eerie "rite of passage." We rode the elevator down, and arriving at the basement, I sent her off with the usual instructions: "Find the stairs and meet us on the third floor."

She hesitated, then said, "I'll do it."

As the elevator door squeezed shut, I shouted, "Good luck,"and then went upstairs to wait with the others.

We waited, and waited. Nothing happened. The aide did not arrive within the expected time, and we began to worry for her safety. Imagining all sorts of disasters—a broken leg, a hit on the head—another nurse and I decided to investigate.

Once in the basement, we called out the aide's name. No response. While the other nurse held the elevator door open, I shined a flashlight around—spotting dusty chairs, boxes and crates. Elongated shadows flickered and fluttered against the walls. I definitely wanted to be somewhere else. I called the aide again, and this time I heard a weak response. I followed the sound of her voice—down one hall, then to the left, finally I located a room. I called to her again.

"I'm here, down here on the floor," she said.

She was in one of the storage rooms, crouched in the corner, in almost total darkness. She told me she had lost her way then became confused and scared. I hugged her and she took my hand. Then I yelled to the other nurse that I had found our missing aide.

As we turned to make our way out of the room, the beam of my flashlight caught something on one of the walls. I thought it was water, but as we looked closer, we saw that it was blood. It was fresh and it glistened in the light. It covered over half of the concrete wall and seemed to be oozing from the wall itself. I could even smell the unique, iron scent of hemoglobin. There was no doubt in my mind—this was blood.

Well, after a scream or two—who's counting—we high-tailed it out of the room toward the elevator.

"Press the button! Press the button!" we yelled to the startled nurse.

When we reached the others upstairs, I told them what we had seen. Everyone got so scared that no one even considered the possibility of returning to the basement—ever.

However, on the following day, after much deliberation, two nurses talked me into taking them to the room where we had seen the blood. Down we went with flashlights in hand—along the dark hallway—my stomach in knots.

We found the room, and I said, "Right in there, on the wall by the door."

We aimed our flashlights, but the wall was dry—clean as sun-bleached bones. There was no trace of blood on the wall or on the floor.

I remember saying, "Let's get the hell out of this place!"

Two days later, I asked one of the maintenance men who had worked in the facility when it was St. Vincent's if he was aware of any strange happenings in the basement.

He told me he had heard stories from other employees but didn't pay them any mind. When I asked him about the room where I had seen the blood, he told me there used to be a small furnace in that room where the hospital surgery department cremated amputated limbs and organs. I just about died on the spot.

As you may have guessed, there have been no more initiations in the basement.

Room 311

About six years ago, when I was working as a Nurse's Aide, I had a weird, ghostly experience during—of all times—the Christmas holiday. I had just finished preparing one of our patients for bed when I heard a crying sound coming from one of the rooms at the opposite end of the hall. I waited to see if another aide was investigating, but when I did not hear anyone approaching, I quickly ran down the hallway, concerned that a patient might have slipped and fallen.

As I neared the room from which the crying seemed to be coming, it suddenly stopped. However, I was sure that it was emanating from room 311, so I opened the door and looked inside. The room was empty.

Then I went from room to room in the general area and checked for the source of the crying. All of the patients were fast asleep in their beds and there was no one on the floor. I thought perhaps a patient had been experiencing a nightmare. I waited in the hallway a few more minutes to make sure everything was in order and then made my way toward the nurse's station.

La Residencia, North View.

The crying began again. It stopped me in my tracks, and I listened carefully. It was a soft, baby-like crying, and it was coming from room 311, the room I had just investigated and found empty.

Immediately, I returned to room 311, opened the door and turned on the lights. The room was still empty. I looked under the beds, thinking a kitten might have found its way into the room, but saw nothing. Nothing that lived or breathed was in that room, but something was in there—for sure. I turned off the lights, closed the door and returned to the nurse's station.

Later the same night, the crying started again. I jumped up, ran to the room and yanked the door open. Immediately, the sound stopped. Either I was terribly scared or mad.

On the following day, I described my experience to another nurse.

"Honey," she explained, "Everyone who has ever worked that third floor has heard that same crying sound. You're not alone with this one! Just forget about it. You'll get used to it."

Later that night, as I was making my nightly bed check, I heard the crying from room 311 again. My patience was wearing thin, but I listened carefully and identified the painful crying as that of a small child. It sounded to me like a child between the ages of three and five. I had once worked directly with traumatized babies and children in the pediatric unit of another hospital, so I soon realized the crying was very much like that of a child gasping for air.

In the pediatric unit, I would at times cradle and rock babies who had been given a terminal prognosis, so I can never erase from my memory the sounds of a baby's last moments of breath —of life—that sad, drawn-out, labored cry. The sound coming from room 311 was that very sound. There was no doubt in my mind the cries I was hearing were the gasps of a dying baby.

It was Christmas Eve, and because of the cold, all the windows were shut tight. I just stood there and listened to the gasping cries as they mingled with the muffled singing of Christmas carolers on the sidewalk below.

I was overcome with sadness at the thought of what might have been the cause of this child's suffering.

Two days later, I was having dinner with a group of colleagues at the hospital, and I brought up the subject of the crying sounds. I expected to be the butt of several jokes, but when I told the women about my experience, they reacted with sincere empathy.

One woman told us that when she had worked at the facility —years ago—when it was known as St. Vincent Hospital, she had been on duty on the third floor pediatric unit during the night shift on Christmas Eve.

"It was Christmas Eve," she said, "and we received an emergency radio call from the state police informing us of a fatal accident on Interstate 25. A father and son were in a two-car collision; the father had been killed instantly, but the little boy had sustained internal injuries. He was still alive—in critical condition. I can still recall the child's little body gasping for breath and his long intermittent cries of pain. I felt so sad watching him suffer and gasp for life."

I asked her which room the baby boy had been admitted to.

"Oh, that was on the third floor, room 311."

Room 311.

The Nurse Assistant's Story: The Call Light

My experience happened about three months ago when I was working on the third floor of La Residencia. One of the patients that I had become fond of expired. Even though she had been very demanding, she had the character of a saint and talking to her was a joy.

But each evening at the same time, she rang the nurse's call bell, and the light above her door turned on. We would always respond and ask what she wanted. Usually she asked for the drapes to be drawn or opened, for a glass of water or for some other small favor, but we all knew she just wanted company—someone to ease her mind until she fell asleep.

I often kept her company and tried to ease her loneliness. However, there were busy nights when her calling would stretched our physical and mental limits. Sometimes, one of the nursing assistants would have to sit with this lady—if the supervising nurse felt it was necessary—and sometimes I was chosen. I sat with her until she fell asleep.

One night, the lady suffered a massive stroke in her sleep and died. The staff nurse noted in her file that she must have died between 11:00 p.m. and midnight since bed checks were conducted on a set hourly schedule. After the coroner arrived, signed the necessary paper work and removed her lifeless body, her bed was changed and the room was made ready for another patient.

We had all come to know her well in the months she was there and felt quite saddened by the news of her death.

The following evening, while accomplishing our various assignments, the nurse's call bell in the lady's room rang, just about midnight. We knew the room was still empty, so we circumspectly looked at each other and at the silently flashing light above her door.

I made the first move to investigate but was soon joined by another nursing assistant. As we opened the door slowly and turned on the lights, we saw nothing out of the ordinary. I reset the call bell and closed the door behind me.

For about a week after that, the nurse call bell and light was somehow activated every night at around midnight. We all knew that this was no coincidence, no electrical malfunction. We agreed that it was the lady's spirit trying desperately to communicate with those who had spent the last days of her life with her.

The following night, when the call bell rang and the light came on, we entered her empty room and softly called out the lady's name.

"Everything's alright dear," we said gently.

I admit I was not sure what would happen next. Nothing did. Since that night, whenever the call bell was activated, one of us went to the room, called out her name to reassure her spirit that everything was okay. Sometime after that, these strange happenings stopped.

Whenever I recall this story, my heart becomes heavy with sadness. I never realized how much I had grown to love this lady until after her death. I guess there is a moral message in this.

I thought the strange happenings were over, but last Thursday night, I heard a loud screaming—sort of a crying sound-coming from room —311. I have heard from other employees that the room is haunted, so I stay as far away as possible from that area.

Clara M. Vigil

The Charge Nurse's Story: Room 311

One of the more frequently haunted areas of La Residencia is room 311, where the disturbances occur so often that administrators try not to place new patients there.

Dolores Trujillo

About the year 1987, I was working the graveyard shift on the third floor. I was busy charting away in the patients' files and answering an occasional phone call. It must have been around 1:30 a.m. when I heard what sounded like a baby crying down the hall. I figured it was probably a cat trying to get in and didn't give it another thought.

But after hearing the crying sound again a few minutes later, I decided to pull myself from the files and investigate. As I got up, I heard the sound again—distinctly the sound of a baby crying. There was no mistake. It was louder and more pronounced. I easily traced the sound down the hall to room 311.

As I approached the room, the sound suddenly stopped. I opened the door cautiously, not knowing what to expect, and reached for the wall light switch. I turned on the light. The room was empty, the mattress bare and the windows shut tight.

If there were a cat, I don't know why it would have chosen such a cold, empty room on the third floor. I was at a loss. I closed the door and went back to work.

Two weeks later, I was with a patient and her husband, and she asked me if I brought my baby to work with me.

"No. Why do you ask?" I said.

"We've both been hearing a crying baby for the past few nights. Poor little thing sounds like it's in an awful lot of pain."

A cold chill went up my spine. Someone else had heard the crying sounds. It wasn't my imagination.

Since that incident, I have not heard the sounds again. I do know several other employees who work the night shift, and we have discussed our experiences with the crying, "ghost" baby.

Footsteps in the Hall

Charge nurse, Dolores Trujillo tells another fascinating story about phantom footsteps heard in the hallways of La Residencia.

~~~~~~~~~~

One night, three nurses and I were gathered at the nurses' station on the third floor. It was approximately 10:30 p.m., and we were discussing patients' medical conditions and internal departmental issues. All of a sudden, we heard the sound of someone running down the hall. We stopped talking and turned in the direction of the footsteps. They sounded like those of a woman in high heels and seemed to be coming from the direction of the west wing. Because I was the closest to the hallway, I went to investigate.

The hall was empty and nothing was out of place. I returned to the nurses' station where everyone was waiting to hear who was the "jogger" in the hall. Just as I was saying I saw nothing, we heard the footsteps again, and they seemed to be headed straight for us. From the echoing, reverberating sound, they were traveling at a very fast pace. Just before it sounded as if they would make contact with the desk, they made a sharp turn and headed left along the south hall.

We just stood there, with eyes and mouths wide open, frozen in time. Then we all knew at the same moment that we had just experienced a ghost. We instinctively reached for each other's hands, trying to gather our composure. Then one nurse made the sign of the cross and prayed aloud for the "thing" to go away. For the remainder of the night, everything was quiet, uneventful.

But a month later things started happening again. One morning, at approximately 4:00 o'clock, I was talking to one of the nurses who had heard the ghostly footsteps. We were sitting behind the nurses' station desk when we heard the familiar footsteps running down the hall.

As they rounded the desk and made their way down the south hall, the other nurse whispered, "Let's follow them and see where they go."

Although her words were courageous, I heard a slight tremble in her voice. I nodded agreement, and as soon as the footsteps passed us, we followed them down the south hall where we ran into another nurse who was coming out of the elevator. We explained our mission and she joined us, but suddenly, the sound of the footsteps ceased.

As the three of us returned to the safety of the nurses' station, we talked about the ghost footsteps and laughed nervously. We had just settled down when we heard the footsteps again. This time we were ready, and we followed close behind like bloodhounds.

When the footsteps approached the stairwell door leading to the basement, they stopped abruptly. I opened the door and we heard the footsteps clicking down the stairs. "That's it," I said. "I'm not going down there. This is as far as I'm going." The nurse who had joined us at the elevator said, "I'm going. I don't believe in ghosts, so if they don't exist, how can they hurt me!"

She got a flashlight and descended the stairs alone. The other nurse and I, too frightened to follow, remained where we were. A few minutes later, the elevator doors opened, and the investigating nurse stepped out... pale and almost in tears.

"My God! What happened to you?" I asked.

"I followed the sound down the stairs, and when I reached the basement, I heard them turn and walk down one of the halls. I followed, and when I reached the end of the hall, I turned to the right and standing there in the darkness, in a doorway, was the figure of a woman with long white hair, wearing a big, dark coat. Although I couldn't see her face clearly, she seemed to be upset. She shook... as if she were sobbing. Then she moved towards me, reaching her hands out to me. I was so scared I turned and ran for the elevator. It was the most awful experience I have ever encountered." Then the nurse broke down and cried and cried.

Immediately, I got on the phone and asked my husband to pick me up as soon as possible.

Other employees have told me they heard the footsteps, but no one had ever had the courage to follow them to the basement.

About a year ago, a nurse's aide, working on the first floor, was near the cafeteria when she heard the sounds of someone walking by the freezer in the closed kitchen area. Thinking it was an employee sneaking a snack without permission, she tried to open the door. It was locked. Then she peered through the glass window of the door. She saw a woman with long white hair wearing a fur coat. In the dimly lit kitchen, she could make out the woman's face. But as the woman passed one of the serving counters, the aide saw that the woman's feet were not touching the floor. The aide left the area immediately and on the following morning, made a full report to the dietary supervisor.

The next morning when the kitchen crew opened the locked door to the kitchen, at first, everything seemed normal. But then, one of the cooks reached down to the floor and picked up what appeared to be several strands of long white hair.

La Residencia strictly follows New Mexico's regulation demanding that at the end of each working day the kitchen floor be swept and mopped. However, from time to time, the kitchen staff will arrive in the morning and discover strands of long white hair on the floor and the counter tops.

Poor Michael

I interviewed Evelina Romero at her home which is located on the west side of Santa Fe. Evelina is divorced and lives with her six year old daughter, two grey cats and a canary. Although Evelina was visibly shaken when recounting Michael's story, she steadfastly assured me that her hope was to prevent such an event from ever happening to someone else. By not presenting any limiting conditions during the interview, Evelina's desires are for the readers of her story to fully comprehend the scope of evil and its all-encompassing nature. The story of Michael which follows, will provide the reader with some of the conviction which Evelina is hopeful for.

Evelina's Story

Michael and I grew up on the south side of Santa Fe. We attended the same schools and worshiped at the same church. Our families got along together well and were regarded as models by the rest of the community. We were wealthy in spirit and values—if not materially. As we developed into young adults, we began to date. At this time, I was about eighteen years old.

After about seven months of dating, I noticed that Michael was acting differently towards his parents and toward me. He had begun to hang around with a new circle of friends who made me feel uncomfortable with their cussing and drinking. They were all from the Cerrillos-Madrid area, about twenty-five miles south of Santa Fe. It seemed as if every time I ran into these guys, they were high on pot or drunk on booze. Michael didn't seem to mind. In fact, he told me that I was too "uptight," that I should try to be more "social."

Needless to say, Michael and I would eventually end up in an argument, so I decided to put our relationship on hold for a while. I felt that Michael was headed in a direction that I did not want to follow, and soon after our split, he indeed gravitated toward these new friends.

As the months progressed, Michael's appearance changed slowly. He let his hair grow, grew a short beard and began wearing "biker" clothes and jewelry—silver skull rings and necklaces with small iron stars or pentagrams and black leather boots. His parents told me that Michael would leave on the weekends with his friends and not return for several days. When he returned from these jaunts, he spent all his time sleeping. He had become rude and demanding toward his parents, and one time threatened to strike his father. Consistently, he yelled that he wanted to be left alone and then storm off to his room. Soon he lost weight, and whenever my parents or I visited him, he was hanging onto a can of beer.

One evening I went to Michael's home to deliver a plate of *biscochos* (cookies) that I had baked. Michael wasn't home, so his mother, grateful for my kindness and aware of our long-time friendship, asked me to speak with Michael and inquire about his strange behavior and long absences. I comforted his mother and told her I would do my best.

Michael's home at 934 Lopez Street.

At that moment, Michael came in and abruptly said, "I'm going away for a few hours. I'll be back in the morning."

He went into his bedroom for a minute and then raced out the door to a carload of waiting buddies. Both his mother and I watched from the kitchen window as the car sped down the road and vanished into the night. His mother looked at me with despair and said softly, "This goes on all the time."

As she shook her head, I said, "He's changed so much. I only hope he doesn't hurt himself."

Michael's mother sobbed then wiped her eyes with the back of her shaking hand. "His father has spoken to him, but Michael thinks he's his own boss now and doesn't want anyone telling him what to do. I'm sure he's smoking pot because I've noticed the smell of something bad burning in his room sometimes."

"Have you been in his room lately?" I asked.

"No. No, I'm afraid of what I'll find."

"Let's go investigate now that he's gone," I said.

She reluctantly agreed.

We opened the door and peered into the darkened room. As I switched on the light, I immediately smelled the harsh pungent odor of burnt oil, a sooty aroma. I noticed clothes and shoes tossed haphazardly about the floor, and posters of naked women and one of the "grim reaper" decorated the walls. On Michael's dresser lay a rusted knife whose handle had been wrapped with a leather strap, numerous colored stones, a partially smoked marijuana joint, and a small statue of Jesus Christ with its head broken off.

His mother said, "Let's leave before he returns."

So we left the room as we had found it.

Several days later, I got a chance to speak with Michael. As usual, he had a beer can in his hand and sipped on it throughout our conversation. When I casually asked what he'd been up to, he told me, without hesitation, that he and his friends were involved in a new religion. I was caught completely off guard but asked him to explain. Being a bit drunk, he openly discussed this new cult he had been initiated into. Basically, he described the symbols used in the religion and left the rest up to my imagination. He rattled off words and sentences about the use of certain colored candles, herbs, and prayers and then the importance of using virgin blood. This was not a bit amusing and my face must have shown it.

Then I said, "Michael, are you a devil worshipper?"

He answered, "I guess you could call me that."

Then he tried to convince me of the "positive virtues" of such a group. We spoke for about an hour; then I tried to show him the negative aspects of the situation he was in, by describing his parents deep distress and sorrow for their son, and how all of this "devil talk" was counter-productive and against the teachings of the Catholic church. He would have none of that. He laughed loudly and told me what a fool I was.

He said, "Don't you want the best things in life? Well the only way to get them is through the 'angel of the morning light.' Don't you see. . . he will listen to whoever calls him!"

For about two weeks, I kept this information to myself. I felt very sad for Michael and his family. And I did not speak to Michael for about two months after that. One day his mother came to my family home and broke down. She cried and admitted that her son needed help. She told us that Michael had gotten drunk the night before, and when his father questioned him about the large bruises and cuts on his arms, Michael had revealed that he was involved with a group of people who practiced a new form of religion, but he said he could not reveal much of the details. However, Michael did admit that he was having doubts about staying with these friends because of what he termed "dangerous practices."

Earlier that evening, Michael had found the courage to confront some of the members of the group and had attempted to terminate his association with the organization, but things had gotten ugly and he was forced to fight his way out. The members of the group had called him a wimp and told him they would kill him if he did not "think twice" about his "unreasonable" decision.

According to his mother, Michael then began to cry uncontrollably. His parents hugged him and eventually he calmed down and swore he would break away from the group.

About a week later, I went to pay a visit to Michael's home. After getting no answer at the front door, I went around to try the back. There I found Michael, sitting cross-legged on the ground, staring at a lit, black candle. Beside him lay the neighbor's German Shephard—dead. Its heart had been cut out of its chest, and Michael was clasping it and holding it above the candle.

"Michael," I screamed, "My God! What have you done to that dog! What are you doing!"

Michael turned to me and shouted, "Get out of here bitch!"

I ran home and told my parents what I had seen. My parents were completely struck with amazement and horror. My mother instructed me not to return to Michael's home and to pray for his salvation. I lit a white candle before the statue of the Virgin Mary and prayed with all my might that Michael would cease his involvement with his "friends". Later that night, around 11:00 o'clock, Michael's mother called, pleading for help, so my mother and I reluctantly went to their home.

When we arrived, Michael's father explained what had happened. When he had challenged Michael about the dog, Michael had told his father that he had to kill the dog with a knife and that he "had to kill animals because this was what he was supposed to do if he were to save his soul." Then Michael had gone to his room and locked the door. His parents decided to try to put their thoughts aside for the night and seek professional help for their son the next day. They had just settled down in the living room when they heard a tremendously loud bang coming from Michael's room. Thinking he may have killed himself, they rushed to the locked door and began pounding on it. From inside the bedroom, they heard Michael's frightened voice pleading, "Don't hit me. Get away from me."

Michael's father pushed, trying unsuccessfully to force the door open. Michael's mother ran and got a clothes iron which they used to smash the lock. Inside, every piece of furniture had been broken or overturned. Clothes and debris were everywhere as if a huge whirlwind had taken complete control. Even the light fixture on the ceiling had been torn off. The mattress was shredded, and clumps of foam from the pillows floated in the air or rested on the destruction. Michael lay unconscious on the floor.

This is when my mother and I arrived. Michael was covered in large bruises and blood. I phoned for the hospital emergency team, and in a few minutes, the ambulance arrived and took

Michael to Saint Vincent Hospital.

That night, recovering in a hospital room, Michael told his parents what had happened. He said after he had gone to his room, he began tossing all the symbols of his new religion—pictures, candles, and other paraphernalia—into his trash can. As he was cleaning his room, he heard a noise at the window, so he looked out and saw what looked like the dark figures of a man and a woman. As he stared at them, the figures, like two huge, winged birds or bats, suddenly entered the room and descended upon him. In raspy voices, they told him that because he wanted to leave the group, he would "pay the price." Before he could call for help, the two beat him unmercifully. The woman hit him first, and then the man hit him. They struck him with hands and wings until he passed out.

On Michael's second day in the hospital, the psychologist placed him on a program of anti-depressants and psychoanalysis to monitor his behavior. It was obvious that the psychologist did not believe Michael's story but thought that Michael was suicidal.

All went well for a few days. Michael seemed to be his old self, and we thought, or hoped, that his problems were over. Then one night, about a month later, we all decided to go out to dinner, but Michael begged off, saying he didn't feel up to it and would be fine at home. When we returned that evening, we found the house in darkness. Michael did not respond to our calls. We proceeded through the house, and I went to the kitchen. There I found Michael, as before, sitting cross-legged staring into a flickering black candle. I called out his name, but he did not answer. Then his parents arrived in the kitchen.

They became extremely upset but called out to him until he responded. He said he was just sitting on the floor and didn't know how the candle got there. His parents decided to re-admit him in the morning. They hugged their son and assured him that everything would be alright. However, they never got the chance. During that September night in 1988, Michael ended his troubles by slitting his own throat. He was 23 years old.

After the funeral, I went with relatives and friends to clean up Michael's room. A priest was called in and blessed the entire house. Michael's parents put the house up for sale and, five months later, moved out.

For awhile, every time the realtor brought potential buyers, the clients complained of an uncomfortable feeling, and some stated that an invisible hand had slapped them. One realtor claims an arm had locked around her neck and pulled her toward the door. For over a year, the house stood empty, unsold.

Today, the house has changed hands, and the interior has been remodeled. The present renter, an artist, told me personally that he has had no unusual experiences.

Sofita Becera

I conducted this interview with Sofita Becera at her home in her living room which also served as her bedroom. The simple items of decoration displayed about her home provided clues to Sofita's modest taste. Handcrafted crocheted doilies and other needlework rested upon Sofita's well-worn furniture. Placed at the foot of her yellow/green sofa was an oblong rug which Sofita's best friend, Belinda Ortiz had given to her as a wedding present many years before.

What remains dominant in my memory, however, was Sofita's religiosity. On a wooden table her deceased husband had made over twenty years ago, stood a statue of the Virgin Mary. In front

Early Photo of Sofita Becera

of the statue was a small bouquet of plastic flowers and a votive candle which flickered continuously throughout the interview.

Born on August 12, 1899, Sofita was nearing 93 years of age but had the spunk and vitality of a much younger woman. She wore thick-lensed glasses because of cataract surgery performed eight years earlier.

Sofita's story concerns a *molcajete*, a carved, stone kitchen tool developed by ancient indigenous peoples several hundred years ago in the valley of Mexico. It is shaped like an average sized melon with the center hollowed out. A smaller stone is used inside the hollowed-out portion of the molcajete to crush or grind herbs and spices. This stone "mortar and pestle" was so useful that it remains a popular tool with people on both sides of the border dividing the United States and Mexico.

Unlike a *metate*—a long, flat stone used by Native Americans throughout the Southwest to grind corn into a flour-like powder—the *molcajete* is rounded, bowl-shaped.

A modern version of a *Molcajete*.

El Molcajete

In 1921, I was twenty-two and had just married Daniel the previous summer. We had a small house about two miles east of the Santa Fe plaza. In those days, two to five miles was not considered very far to travel, and those of us without horses would walk, carrying supplies of food or firewood. It was not an easy life, but the good times made up for the bad.

My good friend since childhood, Belinda Ortiz, would join me at mid-day after I had done the cleaning and fed the chickens and goats. Belinda and I passed the time talking about what was going on in our neighborhood, things like who was romancing who.

During one of these afternoon visits, Belinda and I went outside to rid my yard of a stray dog that was barking and chasing my chickens. Three young neighborhood boys came by, saw our trouble, and started throwing stones at the mongrel.

Once rid of the dog, I asked the boys why they were so covered in dirt. They explained that they had been exploring in the nearby hills and had discovered a small cave behind a grove of trees against the side of the mountain. They had gathered some sticks to enlarge the opening and peered inside. With the help of the afternoon sun, they saw several pots and a quiver of fox pelts containing arrows. I told them they must have uncovered a burial site and should not have touched or taken anything, because they must respect the dead. They listened with wide eyes and then said they did not want to return but were afraid that others might disturb the cave. Belinda suggested they take us to the cave and we could help them cover it up. The boys agreed and off we went.

About six miles into the Sangre de Cristo mountain range, on the eastern edge of the city, we crossed a small stream and entered a grove of trees. There we found the cave. The opening was about four feet high and one foot wide. We peered inside and saw the small painted pots, a woven grass mat, and the quiver of arrows—just as the boys had described. In the back of the cave, I saw a large dark mass of fur and knew this was a burial cave when I saw a bony foot protruding from underneath the fur. I realized that the corpse must have been a man and a hunter because he was wrapped in a bear skin and had his hunt weapons with him, but I kept this knowledge to myself and made the sign of the cross.

I turned to Belinda and the boys and said, "We will have to seal this up, so go down to the stream and bring mud and stones."

While they were all busy at the stream, I looked inside the cave again. This time I saw a roughly carved *molcajete*. I reached in and grabbed the *molcajete* and the small grinding stone that lay beside it. I thought this would fit in my kitchen perfectly, so I carried it some distance away and covered it with grass and leaves. I felt it was worthless compared to the pots or the fox quiver.

We diligently worked with our hastily gathered adobe building materials, and soon the sun had caused a thin crust to develop on the surface of the moistened mud. We placed large branches with lots of leaves in front of the sealed entrance and agreed that we had done a "good job."

I instructed the boys to return home on their own, but Belinda and I stayed behind. After they had gone, I told Belinda about the *molcajate*. She was not very happy about what I had done, but after she saw it, she agreed that it would do no harm to put it to use once in a while, after all those years lying in the cave.

I retrieved the tool and we went home. I scrubbed the *molcajete* clean of all mud and placed it on the kitchen table to surprise my husband. When Daniel saw it, he admired its beauty but asked nothing of its origins. Instead, he suggested I grind some chile for the following day's dinner.

So the next day, I did as he had suggested and crushed some dried, red chile pods for dinner. The *molcajete* performed very nicely, but later that night, while I was sleeping, I was awakened by a loud banging sound. I shook my husband out of his sleep and told him to listen, but the sound had stopped. The next night, I was again awakened by the same sound, but this time I recognized it as the sound one rock makes as it is hit against another—a "click / click" sound. Immediately, I knew it was the *molcajete*. I got goose bumps on my goose bumps, but I kept still and eventually, after what seemed an eternity, the sound stopped.

The next morning I told Belinda about the sounds in the night.

She said it was my own fault for taking what was not mine. I agreed and asked her to return the *molcajete* to the cave. She refused, insisting I should do it myself. But I was too frightened, so I carried the stone to the back of the house and left it there beside the back door.

From time to time, I would hear the familiar sound, but I dared not tell Daniel its history. I just endured the night poundings and the guilt that would overcome me. Out of fear I could not bring myself to return the *molcajete* to its rightful resting place.

One November night, as a soft snow dusted everything, I heard the *molcajete* again. It had been several months since the last time I had heard it, but as usual, the clicking sound awakened me from my sleep. I got out of bed, went to the back door and carefully peered through the window. I saw the freshly fallen snow glistening in the bright light of a full moon. Then I looked down to where the *molcajete* stood and was surprised to see the materialized prints of a barefooted person press into the snow and slowly move away from the *molcajete* until they disappeared behind a large cottonwood tree. Although snow covered everything else in the yard, the exposed *molcajete*, which was

A *Metate*.

being used as a doorstop, had been brushed clean, and the fresh human footprints surrounded the *molcajete*.

Since that night I have heard the clicking sounds of the *molcajete* only twice: on the day that my good friend Belinda died and on the day that Daniel was laid to rest. But I was no longer afraid. I guess I've come to accept the spirit that dwells in or around the grinding stone as something that I will have to live with. I now consider the *molcajete* as if it were a chair or table, something taken for granted but useful when needed. I believe this "stone friend" will stay with me and provide companionship until I leave this world.

Sofita's *Molajete*.

Author's Note: In September of 1991, Sofita suffered a massive heart attack and died at home, surrounded by her son and two neighbors. Later, her son contacted me and informed me that his mother had mentioned to him that she had wanted me to have the *molcajete*. I accepted the gift with nervous apprehension and assured her son that I would take care of it and that eventually I would place it in a location that befits its history.

Historic Taos

There is evidence that man has lived in the Taos area as far back as 3,000 B.C. Prehistoric ruins dating from 900 A.D. can be seen throughout the Taos Valley. The Pueblo of Taos remains the link from these early inhabitants of the valley to the still-living native culture.

The first Europeans to appear in Taos Valley were led by Captain Alvarado, who was exploring the area for the Coronado expedition of 1540. Don Juan de Onate, official colonizer of the province of Nuevo Mexico, came to Taos in July 1598. In September of that year he assigned Fray Francisco de Zamora to serve the Taos and Picuris Pueblos.

Long established trading networks at Taos Pueblo, plus its mission and the abundant water and timber of the valley, attracted early Spanish settlers. Life was not easy for the newcomers, and there were several conflicts with Taos Pueblo before the Pueblo revolt of 1680 in which all Spaniards and their priests were either killed or driven from the province. In 1692 Don Diego de Vargas made a successful military reconquest of New Mexico and in 1693 he returned to re-colonize the province. In 1694 he raided Taos Pueblo when it refused to provide corn for his starving settlers in Santa Fe.

Taos Pueblo revolted again in 1696, and De Vargas came for the third time to put down the rebellion. Thereafter, Taos and most of the other Rio Grande Pueblos remained allies of Spain and later of Mexico when it won its independence in 1821. During this long period the famous Taos Trade Fairs grew in importance so that even the annual caravan to Chihuahua delayed its departure until after the Taos Fair, held in July or August. The first French traders, led by the Mallette brothers, attended the Taos Fair in 1739.

By 1760, the population of Taos Valley had decreased because of the fierce attacks by plains Indians. Many times the Spanish settlers had to move into houses at Taos Pueblo for protection from these raiders. In 1779, Colonel de Anza returned through Taos from Colorado, where he had decisively defeated the Comanches led by Cuerno Verde. De Anza named the Sangre de

Cristo Pass, northeast of present Fort Garland, and also named the road south from Taos to Santa Fe through Miranda Canyon as part of "El Camino Real". In 1796-97, the Don Fernando de Taos grant was given to 63 Spanish families.

By the early 1800's Taos had become the headquarters for many of the famous mountain men who trapped beaver in the neighboring mountains. Among them was Kit Carson, who made his home in Taos from 1826 to 1868. In July 1826 Padre Antonio Jose Martinez began serving the Taos parish. He opened his school in Taos in 1833 and published textbooks for it in 1834. He printed *El Crepusculo*, a weekly newspaper, in 1835 and was prominent in territorial matters during the Mexican and early United States periods in New Mexico.

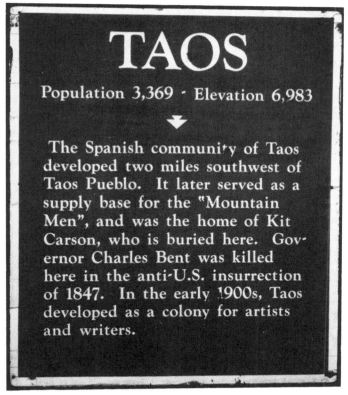

After Mexico gained independence from Spain in 1821, the Santa Fe Trail became the important route for trade between the United States and Mexico. A branch of the trail came to Taos to supply its trading needs.

From 1821 to 1846, the Mexican government made numerous land grants to help settle new sections of New Mexico. During the war with Mexico in 1846, General Stephen Kearney and his U.S. troops occupied the province of New Mexico. Taos rebelled against the new wave of invaders and in 1847 killed the newly appointed Governor Charles Bent in his Taos home. In 1850 the province, which then included Arizona, officially became the territory of New Mexico of the United States.

During the Civil War, the Confederate army flew its flag for six weeks over Santa Fe. It was just prior to this time that Kit Carson, Smith Simpson, Ceran St. Vrain and others put up the American flag over Taos Plaza and guarded it. Since then, Taos has had the honor of flying the flag day and night.

The discovery of gold in the Moreno Valley in 1866 and later in the mountains near Taos brought many new people to the area. Twinging and Red River, once mining towns, are now prominent ski resorts.

The Carson National Forest contains forested lands in the Sangre de Cristo and Jemez Mountain Ranges. It was created from the Pecos River Forest Reserve of 1892, the Taos Forest Reserve of 1906, and part of the Jemez National Forest of 1905.

A narrow gauge railroad, the Denver and Rio Grande Western, was built from Alamosa, Colorado, to twenty-five miles southwest of Taos in 1880. In later years it was nicknamed the Chili Line and eventually connected with Santa Fe. A surrey and four horses joggled passengers from the station to Taos. During World War II, the train was discontinued; Embudo Station on the Rio Grande is all that is left of it today.

The next invasion began in 1898, when two eastern artist came to Taos and depicted on canvas the dramatic mountains and unique peoples. By 1912, the Taos Society of Artist was formed by these and other artist who had been attracted to the area. New Mexico became a state in 1912 as well.

World Wars I and II came and went, and members of the three cultures of Taos—Indian, Spanish and Anglo—fought and died together for their country.

In 1965, a steel arch bridge was built west of Taos to span the gorge 650 feet above the Rio Grande, thus opening the northwestern part of New Mexico to easy access from Taos.

History of the Mabel Dodge Luhan House

Mabel Dodge was born, Mabel Ganson in 1879 into a wealthy and conservative, banking family in the city of Buffalo, New York. She was widowed at age 25 when her husband Karl Evans died. Left with a son John, she married a Bostonian architect Edwin Dodge very soon after. They all eventually left the U.S. and lived in Florence, Italy. Bored with Italy, Mabel decided to return to New York, and bored with her second marriage, she and Edwin divorced. She then married for a third time, an artist Maurice Sterne. Maurice soon left alone for Taos, New Mexico, to "paint Indians". At his urging, Mabel joined him in Taos in 1916. This marriage also did not go well for Mabel and, Maurice returned to New York while Mabel remained in Taos.

In 1929, Mabel bought twelve acres on the edge of Taos, built, and completed her home. The building site location was brought to her attention by a local Taos pueblo Indian, Tony Luhan, whom she later married. Mabel bought the land on June 22, 1918, and paid $1,500 to Manuel de Jesus Trujillo. Existing on the property was a three or four room adobe house. With Tony Luhan's supervision, Mabel built several additions to the small house. Eventually, the house grew to 450 feet in length. When the building was completed, the house had a square footage of 8,440 feet, which included seventeen rooms.

Mabel was known to entertain her Eastern visitors and friends with "colorful" and "charming" Indians of the Taos Pueblo. She had them perform their dances and songs in the dining room.

Mabel's death occurred in 1962. Her son John inherited the house and was unsuccessful in selling it. Mabel's granddaughter, Bonne Bell, lived in the house for about a year, and then moved out. Actor-producer Dennis Hopper bought the house in 1969. For reasons known only to him, he chose not to live in the larger house but, instead, lived in a smaller home owned by the Taos Pueblo. In 1977, the larger house was bought again and used as a learning center for workshops, seminars, etc. Presently, the house is being used as a well-known and popular Bed and Breakfast.

Maria E. Fortin's Story

I've been working at the house since October of 1991. The house is now a Bed and Breakfast of which I am the receptionist and assistant house manager. It's a pleasant place to work because it's quiet, and, aside from the occasional ghost, I enjoy it here very much.

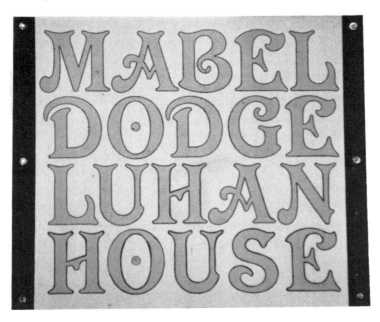

I recall an experience that happened to me about two years ago. It was a nice spring day. At around 3 P.M., I was sitting in my usual chair behind a desk in the reception room. The reception room currently doubles as the B & B gift shop but was, in years past, Mabel's library. In the reception room is located a stairway that leads up to the second floor. There have been several guests who have told me that they have seen a ghostly figure of a woman standing on the stairs. These guests, unknown to each other, have commented that the woman wears a white dress. I knew, from speaking with locals and reading some material on Mabel, that she was fond of wearing white dresses. Some locals at the time nick named her "The Bride" because of her strange but cute custom.

Seated that afternoon in the reception room, I was thinking about what past guests had said about the sightings and was staring at the stairway directly in front of me. Soon, I turned my attention to the paperwork on my desk and opened the reservation book. I was busy checking the information regarding check-ins and such, when I suddenly noticed a faint scent of cinnamon in the air. I turned my attention away from the book and determined that, sure enough, there was a cinnamon smell coming into the room. It quickly enveloped the small reception room. I rose from my chair and walked over to the rear door. There was no hint of anyone or of an opened spice jar. I decided to take a look in the kitchen which was two rooms removed from the reception room, at the north end of the house. Perhaps someone had gone into the kitchen without my noticing them and had decided to bake. Entering the kitchen, I noticed that there was no one around and, strangely, that the scent of cinnamon was not to be found. I thought this was queer. I decided to return to the reception room. As soon as I entered the room, it hit me again. The scent of the spice was so overwhelming, that it made my head spin. Unexpectedly, at that same moment, a woman who conducts tours for visitors to Taos entered the front door and walked over to the reception room. As soon as she entered, her eyes and face lit up with emotional excitement. She took a deep breath and then said, "Mabel is here. Do you smell her presence? She's here right in this room!" I didn't know what this woman was talking about, so I asked her to explain why she was saying these things. She told me that when Mabel Dodge was alive, she enjoyed the smell of cinnamon so much that she always had it around her. She placed small saucers of crushed cinnamon in each room of the house, and hung hand-made potpourris of flowers and cinnamon in the closets and on the door knobs. Apparently, it was an obsession with Mabel. Because of this trait, it was not uncommon for the scent of cinnamon to precede the ghostly apparition of Mable Dodge.

I was unaware of this information, but then I recalled one of the times a guest had told me about seeing the image of the ghostly figure on the stairs. She said that at the time of the apparition she noticed the strong spicy scent of cinnamon in the room. I got quiet and contemplative. Was I about to witness a

Maria E. Fortin

ghost? Was the ghost of Mabel Dodge in the room with me? The though of seeing a ghost overwhelmed me with fear. I got goose bumps on my arms, and the hair on the back of my neck stood on end. All the while, the strong scent of cinnamon lingered in the room.

Soon after, the tour woman left the house. Not wishing to see the ghost, I decided to take a short walk outside, taking comfort in the bright, reassuring light of the afternoon sun. I never got to witness the ghost, but I came pretty close that day.

Since then, I've had guests come up to me and tell me that they have been awakened in the middle of the night by an unknown source and have seen a woman's figure standing before them in their bedroom. She is dressed in a white fabric and slowly disappears into thin air. There also have been other guests who have commented to me that they have been awakened by the song of a Native American. They have gotten out of bed to locate the source of the singing. After a few minutes the singing stops. To say the least, these guests were alarmed by what they experienced. I can't say I blame them. You have to be pretty strong emotionally to see these things. As for me, I'll just wish every one of the ghosts well and hope they keep their distance, at least while I'm on duty.

The house as it looks today.

The Garden Restaurant
Larry C. Tibbetts, co-owner

The restaurant began in this building thirteen years ago. Before that it was an indoor flea market, and before that it was a grocery store. I've personally been associated with the restaurant since it began. Currently, the Garden Restaurant serves breakfast, lunch and dinner and we have a bakery. We're located on the Taos plaza, so it's easy to locate and often a resting point while people are window shopping or strolling through the many stores and galleries. It's also a popular gathering spot for locals and tourists alike.

It was either the first or second day after purchasing the property that I decided to take the stairs down to the basement and look around. I found the usual items that would be found in such an old building, i.e., cardboard boxes, and trash. However, in one corner of the basement there was a cardboard box which, surprisingly, contained a complete human skeleton. Pulling back the cardboard flaps, I could see the rib, hand, spine, leg and arm bones, a disorderly mass of boney framework including the skull. The bones were surprisingly clean although dusty. Apparently, one of the past owners of the building was into archeology. Soon afterward, when the basement was cleaned and all the trash removed, the box which contained the bones was moved to the rear of the basement and forgotten. Two years later, the restaurant changed hands. The new owners, who were devout Catholics, took notice of the box with the skeleton and decided to have a local priest perform a blessing over the bones and bless the building. An archeologist from the local museum was also called in and revealed the origin of the bones. We were told that they were of a Native American woman. For their own reasons, the new owners named the skeleton Snowflake. After the priest was done with his blessings, the box of bones was taken somewhere in town and reburied.

Larry C. Tibbetts

I've not ever had anything spiritual or unusual happen to me here in the building, but employees have. I've been told of strange noises, cold chills and other stuff happening to workers. Our two bakers, Anna and Earl, who spend most of their time in the basement where the bakery is now located, have experienced such strange things.

"Snowflake"
Anna M. Johnson's Story

I have been one of the bakers at the Garden Restaurant now for about seven months. The ghost, or Snowflake as the employees call her, has made her presence known to me in very strange ways. Although I've been scared by her, I want to think she'll never do me any harm. I hope she is a kind and friendly spirit, at least to me. I try to do nice little gestures to show her that I would like to be her friend. For instance, whenever I have any leftover dough, I will bake her her own mini loaf, and place it away from the other employees' view. I usually place it on top of a shelf and in the back away from view. Strangely, when I look for it in a few days, it will be gone. I'll then ask the others about the "missing" bread and they won't have a clue. I make these personal offerings of good will to Snowflake because I don't want her to do anything mean or evil to me. I admit that when I'm

Earl P. White and Anna M. Johnson.

alone in the basement, the last thing I want is to have a nasty ghost watching my every move. Of course I get scared. Who wouldn't? So my little bread loaves for Snowflake are my guarantee that she will leave me alone.

The restaurant's bakery is located in the basement. I know when Snowflake is around because I'll hear strange footsteps on the ceiling above me. When I'm alone down there in the wee hours of the morning, sometimes I'll hear these footsteps. The temperature in the basement reaches between 90 to 100 degrees because of the ovens. Strangely, I'll feel the presence of someone in the basement with me. It's a freaky feeling. Then suddenly, I'll feel this bone-chilling cold wind. I'll become motionless, because I already know this is the sign that the ghost is about. Suddenly, this cold wind will pass right through me! The cold air will last about thirty seconds; then slowly it passes. I experience this about once or twice a week between the hours of 9 p.m. and 5 a.m. If someone speaks of the ghost or mentions her name, it's almost a guarantee that she will give you a dose of cold air. Because I've been talking to you about her during this interview, I know she will become excited and make her presence known to me tonight. I just know it! I'm not the only person who has experienced this. There is another baker named Earl who has heard the noises and felt the cold wind.

A couple of months ago, two other bakers and I were working in the basement when suddenly we all heard the sounds of footsteps coming from above. We stopped what we were doing, and, when the sounds continued, we looked at each other. Then without any more notice we heard a large metal object hit the floor above us. Boy, we were scared! The footsteps continued, only this time we heard a larger metal object being dragged as well. We all knew there was a burglar in the restaurant above us. Then we heard the footsteps become louder and louder. I grabbed a large knife that was on the table, and with the other two employees following behind, we made our way slowly but cautiously up the stairs. We turned on the lights but saw no one. We looked under every table and in each bathroom. Nothing was out of place. The doors were all locked from the inside. Immediately, we knew that the source of the noise was not due to any living person. It had to be Snowflake!

There are other times when I'll be in the basement and I'll hear the pots and pans making all sorts of noise. I'll go into the next room where they are kept on the shelves and hanging on hooks. I'll find several pots thrown over here and pans thrown over there. It's crazy. Sometimes, I'll be busy at work listening to the radio, and then I'll hear a noise, look up and see two, three, or more pans just fly off the rack onto the floor, slide across the room, and end up at the opposite wall!

I know there are such things as ghosts. If I didn't know before, I sure do now. I get scared sometimes when I'm alone in the restaurant. Although Snowflake has scared me, I know she is just upset because of all the years her bones were kept unceremoniously in a cardboard box. Her spirit must be trapped within the walls of the restaurant. I just hope she finds rest and peace someday.

Earl P. White's Story

I've been baking for the restaurant now for over a year and a half. There have been mornings that I've been in the basement between 1 and 3 a.m., baking cookies and such, when I've heard thuds and footsteps on the floor above me. At first, I was just annoyed, but soon I became more and more frightened due to the history of the skeleton in the basement.

I've felt the cold wind that Anna has spoken about. The bakery in the basement has no windows, so when this cold wind approaches, you can feel it for sure! It's been my experience that when the footsteps begin upstairs, the cold wind will surely follow down in the basement. It's difficult to regard this stuff as normal. I sometimes work alone, so I don't want to encourage the ghost to visit me. The whole subject makes me uncomfortable.

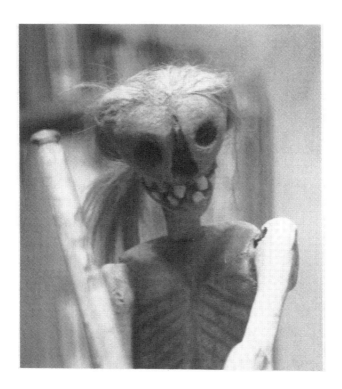

History of the Hacienda Martinez

In October of 1983, over 250 descendants of Antonio Severino and Maria del Carmel (Santistevan) Martinez gathered at the hacienda to celebrate the opening of their ancestral home as a museum. The Hacienda had been continuously occupied by members of the family until 1931. The Hacienda represents not only the cultural heritage of the Martinez family but is a living expression of the continuity and vitality of the Spanish colonial pioneering frontier spirit of northern New Mexico.

The term *Hacienda* may be a misnomer for the structure as the designation in New Mexico is more appropriately applied to the large, early colonial period constructions of the seventeenth century which were built by and dependent on, for the most part, forced Indian labor. After the Reconquest the primary form or unit of settlement became the *rancho*, a term common in northern New Mexico for a more modest self sufficient establishment of one or more households. The designation "hacienda" does not seem to have been customarily used in this area again until the

coming of the Americans in the first quarter of the last century. At the time of Severino's death in 1827, his sons, Padre Antoino Jose and Santiago Martinez referred to the home in written documents as a *casa mayor*, or great house (could be old house as well). Regardless, locally the Martinez family's casa mayor has come to be known as the Martinez Hacienda, although, to be more correct in Spanish it should be *Hacienda Martinez* or *La Hacienda de los Martinez*.

Other terms that have come down to us from the Spanish colonial period which could also be appropriate include: "restricted plaza" and *casa-corral*. The restricted plaza identifies a single extended family occupied fortified compound containing a small plaza or placita. Casa-corral is perhaps an even better designation as it is defined as a placita surrounded by living quarters, storage areas and rooms for entertaining, and this all attached to a second placita or walled corral area which may or may not have had additional rooms for servants or slaves and enclosures for animals, supplies and tack. There are no indications in the historic record to determine if the second placita or walled corral was constructed in Severino's time or added later by one of his heirs. However, based on the fortress-like construction of the first placita, it seems reasonable, that Severino would have built a walled corral for the protection of his animals as well.

Restoration of the Hacienda

From 1804 until 1931, the Hacienda was owned by members of the Martinez family. With the death of Severino Martinez, in 1827, the Hacienda passed to his wife and children, and when Maria del Carmel died two years later the entire estate transferred to the children and their spouses. The youngest son, Pascual Bailon Martinez eventually acquired sole possession of the Hacienda. Pascual continued to increase the family's land holdings while maintaining extensive ranch and trade operations which extended to Chihuahua in the south and St. Louis to the east. Pascual died in 1882 and the hacienda remained with his heirs until 1931.

Each generation of the Martinez family made untold changes to the building by adding and enlarging windows and doors, and altering interior and exterior spaces to meet the needs of the new families and the changing times. In the early years of the twentieth century Taos Society of Artists member Eanger Irving Couse rented a portion of the Hacienda from the Martinez family and had a huge north facing window installed for his studio.

The hacienda began to fall into disrepair around the time of the Second World War and was little more than an abandoned

ruin in 1964 when Jerome and Anne Milord purchased it and started a major restoration project of the structure. The Milords were unable to complete the work and in 1972 sold the Hacienda to the Kit Carson Memorial Foundation, now known at the Kit Carson Historic Museums.

With the assistance of historians, archaeologist, historic preservation architects and the descendants of Severino and maria del Carmel Martinez, the Foundation, under the leadership of Director Jack Boyer, began the extradorinarily ambitious project of restoring and furnishing the Hacienda to the 1820's period when it was occupied by Severino and his family. One of the most important contributions to the restoration was a historic document, the "Last will and Testament of Don Severino Martinez." The Will and associated probate documents provided a detailed accounting of virtually all of Severino's belongings and their relative value as well as the number and size of many of the rooms within the great house. Through these documents we are able to view the material culture and to appreciate the lifeways of the late Spanish colonial and early Mexican Republic periods of Taos.

The Hacienda Martinez today is a restoration. Sincere attempts were made from the beginning of the project to recreate the atmosphere and character of the early part of the nineteenth century. As future research and scholarship reveal new information about this special place the Museums will continue the interpretation and restoration process. Additional alterations will be made to reflect the new findings in an effort to more accurately represent the site and times. This ongoing process of interpreting and authenticating will give visitors a better understanding and appreciation of the historical and cultural development of northern New Mexico.

Elma Torres' Story

I've been working at the Hacienda Martinez now for seven years. When I began, I was the receptionist and now I'm currently the head receptionist.

I'm not the kind of person who welcomes ghostly experiences

or expects any unusual happenings or apparitions. That's why I was left with such a feeling of shock when I had my experiences at the Hacienda. I'm hoping that the spirits I encountered at the Hacienda are friendly to me. After all, I'm still working at the house and I don't want to upset anyone living, or especially anyone dead. I'm hoping that if I ever have another encounter, I'll be able to deal with it, but who knows?

Elma Torres

My first experience at the Hacienda took place during one October evening. It was around 5 p.m. I remember that I had been employed for three years and till then, had never had any unusual ghostly encounters. I had heard from other employees and grounds keepers, that strange things did go on at the old adobe compound, but I didn't pay their stories too much attention.

Well, that evening it was quite cold, and all the tourists had left the property hours before. I was seated in the bookstore / entrance area browsing through one of the many books that are sold at the Hacienda. I was just passing the time until the 5 o'clock hour when I could go home. I began to hear some noise directly outside the front door. I placed the book I was reading down on the desk and waited for the knob to turn and for a tourist or two to enter. I heard the sounds of someone moving about and the shuffling of feet. I waited for the door to open, but no one came in. Thinking whoever it was had changed their mind about entering, I glanced at the clock and picked up my book and began to read. About fifteen minutes later, once again I heard someone outside the entrance door. I could clearly hear the shuffling of shoes and other sounds which indicated to me that there was someone on the other side. I placed the book on the desk, rose from my chair, and made my way to the door. I placed my ear to the door in an attempt to hear a voice, but I heard nothing. I took hold of the knob, gave it a strong pull, and opened it wide. Expecting to see someone, I was quite surprised to see I was alone. There was no wind, just the stillness and cold of the fall evening. I took a few steps, looked around the building, but saw no one. What could it have been? I don't have a clue, but I know that I heard someone. I just know it! Was it a ghost? You tell me. What else could it have been?

The following year, also in October, I was closing up the Hacienda. All the tourists had left and I was making my usual rounds, making sure all the doors and windows were locked. I made my way through each room. I then went outside and proceeded to the breezeway that connects the first courtyard to the second. As I made my way through the breezeway, I immediately felt the presence of a person close to me. I naturally stopped and turned to face the person. There was no one visible to me. Then I thought to myself, how odd that I would sense such a thing. I tried to disregard this strange feeling and once again took a few steps towards the direction of the second courtyard. I found that the overwhelming feeling of someone standing next to me was too strong to ignore anymore. At this point, I heard the footsteps on the gravel of someone rushing up to my right side. I froze and then suddenly I heard the deep, hard breathing sounds that someone makes as they inhale then exhale a breath of air.

I actually felt the breath on my neck! I don't know what snapped inside me, but at that point I quickly turned around and dashed to the front office. I didn't care if the remainder of the building was not secured and locked. I had just one thing in mind: to get the heck out of there! I managed to turn off the main light switch, lock the front door and get into my car. I'll never forget this experience. I was told some time after this that several people have seen and have heard a woman crying in one of the rooms. We've even had a medium or psychic, walk through the room who has told us that the woman is definitely very sad about something. Some workers have seen this ghost woman walk by the windows, as the employees watch from the outside. I get goose bumps just hearing their stories. Although, I've not

"I heard the footsteps on the gravel..."

seen this woman's spirit, there have been times that I have been leisurely walking through the Hacienda and I have seen shadows. It can be day or night. I've noticed the silhouette, or shadow-like presence of someone either looking at me from a window or walking past a door. I know what I've seen is real. I even saw the outline of a person's head facing me from a window.

All these things have given me, over time, the emotional toughness and energy to simply deal with the ghosts. They haven't hurt me, so, since I don't talk bad about them, I hope they keep their distance.

Another employee had an experience when she was also alone at the Hacienda one night. Her name is Dolores. She really got scared at the time. It seems that strange things happen to us when we are alone and towards the end of the day. That's just the way it is, I guess.

Dolores I. Struck

I began working at the Hacienda on February 1993. My present position is receptionist/clerk. I was born and raised in Rancho de Taos.

It was a cold October evening, and the time was 5:30 p.m. I was at the Hacienda and was alone. I was counting the money and totaling up the day's receipts from the admissions and book sales. Suddenly, I heard a man's voice singing or humming outside the front door. The sound he was making made me think he was very happy about something. It was loud and joyous. I stopped what I was doing and went to see if there was a tourist that had lingered too long and was locked out. I opened the door, looked around, and didn't see anyone. I'm not sure why this affected me so negatively, but I got scared. I wanted to get out of there fast. I was very sure that what I had heard was not my imagination. I know it wasn't. I hadn't heard this singing before, so I was scared.

Another experience that I've had at the Hacienda is the feeling that someone is staring at me. I feel someone's eyes just watching me. This always happens unexpectedly. Just out of the

Dolores I. Struck

blue, I feel someone's glaring eyes watching me. I turn around and there is no one; I am all alone in the room.

People have told me about a crying woman ghost in one of the rooms. I haven't seen her, but people have heard her crying.

There are other incidents that have happened to me in the first courtyard area. When I've gone from room to room, closing and locking up the windows and doors for the evening, I've returned to discover three of the windows wide open. Could it be the wind? Maybe, but I don't want to talk about this anymore. I just hope its a friendly ghost.

The Stables Art Center

The Stables Art Center was once the home of Arthur Rochford Manby, an Englishman, who came to New Mexico in 1883 to seek his fortune. It was in this house that his headless body was found on July 3, 1929.

In April, 1898, Manby bought seven parcels of land [about twenty-three acres] just north of Kit Carson's home and the old wall of Taos, and east of the public road to the Taos Pueblo.

Manby had been trained as an architect in Belfast, Ireland, and promptly set about designing and building his enormous Spanish-style hacienda of nineteen rooms set in a square with three wings, stables, and outer walls. The adobes were made in the back pasture (Kit Carson Park); timber and vigas were cut and hauled from the nearby mountains. In 1907, the house interior was described by visitors as having rough plank floors, spruce rafters and walls plastered with tierra blanca.

The house was furnished in 1907 with English furniture of walnut and mahogany, old Spanish chests and fine oil paintings, one of which secured the future of the house. A 1904 photograph shows Manby seated in a wicker chair in front of the kitchen fireplace where an iron teakettle hangs over the fire.

When Mabel Dodge Sterne arrived in Taos in December 1916, she immediately applied to rent the "largest and most attractive house in town". She agreed to pay $75.00 a month rent and Manby moved into the west wing of the house.

Soon Mabel moved out of the home and not long after, Manby died in 1929. His death created "the greatest unsolved mystery of the west".

The property then passed to Dr. Victor Thorne, a wealthy New York art collector, who had purchased one of Manby's paintings, a Vandyke. Dr. Thorne also held a second mortgage on the property which he thought might become a summer home for his family. In 1936, he sent Miss Helen Williams to Taos to discover the condition of the house. She arrived to find the roof fallen in, squatters in some of the rooms, the front porch fallen down, and the windows all broken out. She wrote to her employer that the place was beyond repair, "absolutely ridiculous", but he sent instructions to go ahead with the project anyway.

Dr. Thorne never did get to Taos. When he died suddenly without leaving a will, Miss Williams continued to respect his wishes, renamed the home Thorne House, and opened it as a community center. Religious groups met in Thorne House, brides held their receptions there, and music lovers gathered in the gardens to listen to each other's records.

Inevitably, with the passing years, Helen Williams aged. Her desire to see Thorne House remain to serve the public found an appropriate solution in Emil Bisttram's dream of a museum and gallery for the artists of Taos. The Taos Artists Association, now known as the Taos Art Association, was founded. In 1952, they purchased the Thorne property-house, lilac garden, stables, and three acres to the east-for $45,000, at one-half of one percent interest.

The house was quickly turned into a museum and then the artists tackled the stables. They tore down the stalls, cemented the floors, and plastered inside and out. The outside doors were left in place, huge doors which could be opened in good weather.

The museum proved to be too difficult for amateurs to manage; all of the borrowed treasures were returned to their owners. For a decade, Thorne House held the newly founded Millicent Rogers Museum, until it could expand into a home of its own seven miles north of Taos. Then came Del Sol, a weaving cooperative, whose members were reviving the old weaving traditions of northern New Mexico.

Finally, in 1972, the president of the Taos Art Association made the decision to move the gallery from the stables into the front house.

People always asked the docents, "In which room was Manby's body found?". There were two adjacent bedrooms in the front of the house. His head was found in one and his body was located in the other.

As we recognize it today, Arthur Rochford Manby's house became the Stables Gallery.

Authur R. Manby House Chronology

1898	In April, Arthur manby bought the land and began to build this hacienda, his home.
1907	Manby had furnished his house with English pieces in walnut and mahogany, old Spanish chests and fine oil paintings.
1919	In December, Mabel Dodge Sterne agreed to rent the "largest and most attractive house in town" from Manby for $75.00 a month.
1921	Mabel Dodge Luhan moved into her own home.
1929	On July 3, Manby's headless body was found in the house.
1936	Helen Williams arrived to refurbish the Manby house for Dr. Thorne.
1938	First central heating in Taos installed in Thorne House.
1940	Thorne House opened as a community center.
1952	Thorne House and 3 acres of land to the east purchased by Taos Art Association.
1953-57	TAA Museum-period rooms furnished from local collections.
1958-68	Millicent Rogers museum collection displayed in Thorne House. Del Sol weaving cooperative in the building.
1972	The Stables Gallery moved from the stables into the house.
1980	The structure of the TAA changed, making this the Stables Art Center.

Vikki E. Madden's Story

I've been working here for one-and-a-half years. I began working here in February 1994. I'm a jeweler and my present position is gift shop manager.

Prior to my employment, no one mentioned anything about the place being haunted. However, after three months of working at the gallery, people became more comfortable about speaking of strange and unusual occurrences. I didn't even know the history of the building or of Mr. Manby.

My experience happened on July 1994 at 6:30 p.m. I was closing the shop and had made sure that everyone was out of

Vikki E. Madden

the gallery and gift shop. I heard some sounds coming from the back office, and I thought that was strange because I had made sure everyone was out. The sounds I heard were of someone walking on the floor boards. You know, heavy footsteps. This is an old building, and the floors are original. It's difficult for anyone to sneak up on someone simply because the old floors are so noisy. I suspected that someone was in the back office and was walking about. I decided to investigate. I looked about the rear of the gallery where the offices are located and, not finding anyone, I decided to leave. I turned and as I approached the front door, I heard the unmistakable sounds of footsteps once again. I had to satisfy my curiosity, so I returned to the rear office area. I thought that perhaps someone was hiding and playing a trick on me. I turned on all the lights and inspected behind every door and under every desk. I have to admit that soon after I was feeling pretty creepy. I decided to leave once more and just as before, when I reached the front of the gallery, I heard the footsteps once again. At this point I did feel scared. Slowly, I made my way to the rear of the gallery and turning on the lights, I noticed

"On the floor were fresh dog paw prints."

on the floor of one of the rear rooms were fresh dog paw prints! I stopped down on one knee to take a closer look. Yes, indeed, I thought, these prints were definitely not here before. Using one of my fingers, I reached out to touch one of the prints. It was of a medium size dog, formed from dirt, and it was fresh!

I got up, looked about the room, and rubbed my arms. They were covered in goose bumps. I quickly turned off the lights and swiftly made my way to the front of the gallery and locked the door behind me.

When I returned the following morning, I decided not to mention my previous night's experience for fear that I would be seen as a "wacko". The morning's bright light gave me the courage I needed to once again visit the floor where the prints were. They were gone! Since I was the last person to leave and the first one to enter in the morning, I was upset by the whole experience. I have been told by people that Mr. Manby owned a dog which went everywhere with him. An eerie feeling comes over me, at times, when I'm here at the gallery.

I mean, the owner's headless body was found in this very room several years ago. This is reason enough for me to believe that some negativity is still around, wouldn't you agree?

"Gramps"
Bobbie A. Gonzales

I'm a firm believer that life goes on after our physical bodies have been laid to rest. I know this to be a fact. As you hear my personal story, you too may come to believe that as well.

Bobbie A. Gonzales

My story is not scary or morbid, it is, instead, a personal story of the love I had and still hold for my grandfather Jesse Parra.

Gramps was born in 1905. As a child, I always sought attention from Gramps. I loved his warm hugs and caring face. I know now how fortunate I was to know the warmth of my grandfather's love. I respected and honored him for simply being Gramps.

As an adult, I always made it a point to make contact with him each day. Gramps lived in his own place with his little dog Senior. I would either pay him a daily visit or give him a phone call just to let him know I had not forgotten him. Many evenings I would walk with Gramps and Senior, taking in the fresh air and beautiful sunsets for which Taos is famous. When I arrived at Gramp's townhome, he would proudly bring out a fresh bowl of his homemade salsa which we both quickly finished off.

Jesse Parra "Gramps"

One day I convinced Gramps to take a short vacation to visit my brother and sister in San Francisco. While Gramps was off in California, I decided to shampoo the rugs in my home. Since the rugs were wet, I thought it would be best to spend a couple of days at Gramps' place until they dried out. At the same time I could watch over Gramps' little companion, Senior. I phoned and spoke to Gramps who described in detail all the fun he was having in Northern California. One portion of the conversation I clearly recall was his enjoyment in describing how much he loved walking on the sea shore, collecting sand dollars and shells. He also spoke about attending a football game and eating ice-

"There in the dim light I saw the image."

cream with his nephew. The following day everyone, including Gramps, was to rise early and go deep-sea fishing. His voice was filled with excitement, and I was so very happy to know things were going well. We ended our conversation with "I love you".

That evening as I slept soundly in Gramps bed with Senior by my side, I was awakened. I slowly opened my eyes and turned to see what time it was. The clock marked the hour at 4 a.m. I sluggishly sat up in bed and without any clear thought gazed toward the hallway. There in the dim light I saw the image of my grandfather. Without pausing to make sense of the moment, I accepted what I was viewing as being my grandfather. He was dressed in his usual flannel shirt, a white tee-shirt and brown pants. I was not alarmed, I just absorbed the moment, so to speak and peace came over me. I saw Gramp's little dog Senior by the bed viewing everything, but not a wimper did he make. He just seemed to take everything in stride. When I returned my eyes to Gramp's image, I saw Gramps extend his arm, and turn his hand palm up, and then slowly raise it level to his waist. For an unknown reason, I realized the message that Gramps had successfully conveyed to me. Gramps had died, and he had come back to say good-bye. At that moment when I knew the purpose of his visit, his spirit must have known I understood, because the image of my grandfather then slowly began to fade away. I was left with a serene peace. The world was a beautiful place at that moment. A smile came over my face. The silence was broken when only four minutes had past, and the phone by the bed rang. When I placed the receiver to my ear, I heard my mother's voice. Before she could say another word, I stated, "Grampa died didn't he?" She said yes, and that he had died of a stroke in his sleep.

Gramps was laid to rest in Santa Fe. Whenever I think back to the days we shared together I feel sad and long for his company. But my grief doesn't last very long because I know that even though death is a powerful force, it can't conquer love.

Windsong Gallery
Wendy Wysong's Story

When I moved into the building in July 1994, I could clearly see that the place needed major work and a loving touch. Apparently, a lot of rain water had destroyed most of the wooden floor planks, so I proceeded to make the floor my first priority when I remodeled. I removed the rotted planks and replaced them with new wood. During this process, I also re-mudded the old scruffy, adobe walls which were water damaged, too. I'm proud to say that I turned the building into something I'm proud of. Currently, I'm leasing and using the building as a business. A portion of the building is a gallery in which I sell local religious art-Santos, retablos, etc. I also try to feature local jewelers' work and Native American art. Directly above the gallery on the second floor is located my personal living quarters. Outside the gallery building is my other business-a espresso bar named Teo's, where I sell various fresh pastries and coffees.

From what has been told to me, the original structure, which is over 300 years old, was part of a fortress that predates the St. Francis Church, which is located just a few yards away. I was surprised to learn that the building I'm in used to be a part of a long, massive wall which connected all the buildings that surround the present day church. The wall took a large rectangular shape which also followed the present highway to the West. Apparently, men used the top of the wall as a lookout for Comanche and Ute Indians, who made raids on the compound day or night.

The original owners of the compound were the Arragon family. A more recent descendant of the Arragon family was a man named Timoteo. After Timoteo's death, a Texas couple bought the property and soon sold it to the present owners in 1994. Timoteo's brother Pedro, or Pete lived with him. Pete had a small adobe building behind the house which he used as a barber shop. Before the death of these two brothers' mother, she had requested

Wendy Wysong

that her older son, Timoteo, look after his younger brother Pete. Both brothers lived in the portion of the building that's presently the gallery, until Pete's death. Pete died upstairs in the second floor above the gallery showroom in 1986. Sometime later, when Timoteo was eighty-five years old, he himself became very ill and was taken by his nephew to live with his family in Denver, Colorado. Sadly, while in his care, Timoteo died. In Mr. Timoteo Arragon's honor, I decided to name my espresso bar, Teo's.

Well, early one evening after closing up the gallery for the night, I went upstairs to prepare dinner and settle in for the evening. Trying to decide what to prepare for dinner, I opened the pantry doors and walked inside. I stood there, and determining what I wanted, I reached for a can on the shelf. Suddenly, the door behind me closed with such a force that I was pushed into the shelves of cans and dry goods. I immediately assumed there was someone who had walked into the gallery and come upstairs. Perhaps a friend had attempted to play a strange joke on me. I turned, and moved away from the pantry, looked around the room, and then quickly went outside. I saw no one. There was nothing available that would explain what I had just experienced in the kitchen. I heard no footsteps running away. I was left with a feeling of bewilderment. I soon realized that there was something more to this experience. I didn't feel that it was a negative force, mean or evil, given what it did to me, but rather more like a wake-up call. I took it to mean that a spirit was responsible, possibly Pete or Timoteo. I believe that the spirit wanted to make itself known to me; in other words, I felt as if this entity wanted me to know it was not gone but was still the caretaker of the building.

I have two cats which I brought to live with me in the building. These cats have noticibly become very nervous and strange in their habits. For instance, they are now up all night, and with any small, insignificant noise they jump and turn sharply towards the direction of its source. It's weird to see. I don't see or hear anything at all, but apparently they see something very important to them. I've found them both looking up at the ceiling for several minutes at a time. They just stare and stare.

To be sure, my ghostly experiences here in the building have made me more aware of my surroundings and of the unique

Señor Timoteo Arragon

quality of this area in Taos. I'm now tuned into the sensibility that I've developed in the short time I've lived here. I'm aware of a presence which is looking out at me, hopefully as a protective force. I can sometimes feel the eyes of someone's stare or the physical presence of someone standing close to me. It's not a negative feeling; I just get the impression that "it" wants me to know it's here in the building with me. I guess because of the positive manner in which I've gone about remodeling the property, keeping the original owners in mind, the spirits are thankful for my sensitivity. There is so much in the way of new construction that is closing in on the property, I'm sure the old ones who took pride in their land and traditional way of life might be upset about it all. I'm not much surprised that their spirits may not at all be happy to learn how we, the living, go about making changes to areas that have been doing just fine for centuries

History of Taos Pueblo

Taos Pueblo, home of the Taos-Tiwa Indians, is the site of one of the oldest continually inhabited communities in the U.S. Taos Pueblo is the northernmost of New Mexico's nineteen pueblos; it is located seventy miles north of Santa Fe, the state capital, two miles north of the world famous art colony of Taos, and some fifteen miles from the internationally renowned Taos Ski Valley. The Pueblo is at an elevation of 7,000 feet.

The origin of the Pueblo in its present form goes back many hundreds of years before the Spanish arrived in 1540. It goes back some 300 years before Marco Polo traveled to China in the 13th century. Had Columbus discovered the "new" world even 500 years before he did, back when Europe as we know it was young and "America" was not even a vision, and had he proceeded immediately to the great Southwest after stepping ashore on a remote island off the Atlantic Coast, he would have found in place in Taos a vibrant and established culture. The Pueblo was here long before Europe emerged from the Dark Ages and made the transition from medieval to modern history.

A regiment of Spanish Conquistadors from Coronado's 1540 expedition were the first Europeans to see Taos Pueblo. The Spaniards reportedly were in quest of the Seven Cities of Cibola (the fabled cities of gold) and they believed they had finally found one of the cities of gold when they saw Taos Pueblo from afar, perhaps with the sun shining upon it. What the Spaniards saw was not a city of gold but two massive, multi-storied structures made of shaped mud and straw and with soft, flowing lines which came to be the distinctive architectural style of the entire Southwest. Taos Pueblo looked very similar to the way it does now, divided into north and south houses by the westerly flowing Rio Pueblo de Taos.

In 1680 a massive revolt against the Spanish was conceived in Taos and launched successfully by the united effort of all the pueblos. The Spanish were driven back into Mexico and all of the territory of New Mexico, including the Spanish capital of Santa Fe, was again in Indian hands. This was an event truly distinctive in the annals of American Indian resistance to the opening of the "new world". It remains today the only instance where extensive territory was recovered and retained by Native Americans, through force of arms.

Taos, the seat of the rebellion, returned to its traditional, full independence for a period of almost two decades. The Spanish returned in 1693 with a large army, but Taos itself remained the center of open rebellion for some five years after the southern pueblos were once again subjected to foreign control. This distinctive military success is especially noteworthy in light of the fact that it was achieved by the traditionally peaceful, agrarian-based pueblos, a tranquil society that initially welcomed the foreigners with open arms.

The pueblo's native religion and culture survived not only the turmoil of the last decade of the 17th century—a hundred years before the birth of the United States of America—but also the 1847 rebellion of the pueblo against the new American government that replaced the Mexican, and other centuries of Spanish, Mexican and American dominance. Taos Pueblo has retained its old ways to a remarkable degree.

The rich cultural heritage of the pueblo is exemplified not only in the exquisite architecture but also in the annual seasonal dances. Visitors to the pueblo are welcomed to observe the dances, but are not allowed to take photographs of them.

The current reservation economy is primarily supported through the provision of government services, tourism, arts and crafts, ranching and farming. In 1980, the tribal council established a Department of Economic Development to generate tribal revenue and job opportunities and to assist local Indian businesses. Many opportunities for development are available to the pueblo, some of which include increased capitalization of tourism, labor-intensive clean-industry plants, and office rentals.

Alfred J. Montoya's Story

I was born on the Taos Pueblo Reservation in 1950. The beautiful mountains which surround the pueblo are the Sangre de Cristos (Blood of Christ). They were given this name by the Spanish because, during some sunsets, the light that reflects from the sky onto these mountains colors the mountains red. These mountains are sacred to the pueblo people and are always honored in a very special way. I always enjoy hiking into the mountains and being at peace with our Mother Earth. I do some hunting of deer, elk, bear and a lot of fishing. As a member of the pueblo, I don't need a hunting license to hunt these animals; however, outside of the pueblo land it's required. I prefer to stay here in our mountains where I feel free to do as I wish without restrictions. It was in these sacred mountains where I had my first experience with spirits.

Alfred J. Montoya

In the fall of 1974, I was employed by the forest service. My job duty was to clean up areas where irresponsible hikers and campers had tossed paper, bottles, cans and other trash in the forest. The crew of guys I was with used horses to travel about the area. One day we were instructed by our supervisor to ride up to Blue Lake, which lay deep within the mountains, and clean up the area. I was busy with some other work at the time and was excused from heading out early. The others in my crew, including my supervisor, left in the morning, and I was to meet up with them later in the afternoon.

Eventually I reached the lake at about 3:30 P.M. that afternoon. I scouted the area and spotted horse tracks and footprints all about the ground. I knew that the crew had done their job of cleaning up the area, so I decided to head-out in the direction the crew might be in order to meet-up with them. I had been instructed by my supervisor earlier that day to locate and follow an old, crude, barbed-wire fence. By following the fence, I would travel in the direction the men would be going. This was a shortcut route. I gazed above the mountain tops and noticed that the clouds were traveling fast. The cold night would soon come, so I attempted to hurry as best I could. Luckily, I had packed a few food supplies and a bed-roll on my horse before leaving for the mountains. All I knew was that my destination where I would meet the others was what we called in our pueblo language "place of the onion grass".

Ultimately, I did locate the barbed wire fence. It branched out in two directions; one went east, the other west. I sat on my horse for a few minutes, trying to decide which way to go. Trying to make sense of everything was difficult, especially since the forest was pretty thick with growth. I decided the best option was to follow my instincts and go what I thought was north. I began to notice that things were not right. I knew I was getting lost because, after about five miles of riding, I began to travel down a ridge which was unfamiliar to me. To make matters worst, the sun would soon be giving way to the night, so I needed to locate my friends.

Before long, I reached an area that I recognized from other previous visits to the area. Immediately I knew I had gone too far and had missed the trail. I reached a stream and followed it north, I needed to hurry because the sun was now behind a ridge and a cool breeze was settling in. Suddenly I turned to my right and I saw a beautiful big buck, about a ten pointer! The buck had his head lowered and was drinking from the stream. My horse made a noise, and the buck raised his head. He faced my direction and I could see his big, dark eyes gazing at me. I always carried a pistol with me, so when I saw this buck out in the open, I knew the opportunity for fresh deer meat was just a few feet away from me. I slowly reached for my gun, brought it into my line of sight, and had the buck in my view. Something inside me made me lower the pistol. I decided not to shoot. I put my pistol away and then looking right at those big black eyes, I held up my hand and in the Indian way said, "Good-bye my brother. We will meet again someday". As I rode my horse away, I took a short glance behind me and noticed the buck just stared at me as I rode away. I soon reached the meadow area known as "the place of the onion grass". Since it was already dark, I thought it would be best to make camp for the night. I could join up with my buddies in the morning. It didn't take long for me to make a fire and roll out my sleeping bag. I led my horse a little way to a grassy area of the meadow and left him to graze for the night.

It was definitely a dark night. As I ate some of the food I had brought with me, I gazed up at the stars and felt at peace. I asked the Creator and Mother Earth to protect and watch over me. I threw more wood on the fire and listened to the cracking and snapping noises it produced as the wood was consumed. I rose from where I was seated and went to get my horse. I returned to the camp and tied my horse close to where I could keep an eye on him. Throwing more wood into the fire, I decided to make some coffee. There I was in the cold darkness with both hands wrapped around my coffee mug. Everything was peaceful and soon I felt sleepy enough to climb into my sleeping bag for the night. I watched the fire dance before me and very soon my eyelids became heavy. Before I closed my eyes, I heard some noise to my right. I sat up within the sleeping bag and turned my head in the direction of the noise.

"He came closer and I kept still."

The flickering light of the fire illuminated the area I was looking at. There from the forest came into view a man dressed in old, traditional-style, Indian garments. He was dancing but had his back towards me. He came closer and I kept still. He had an odd manner of dancing which I was not familiar with. Soon he was opposite the fire from me. Although I heard no music, no drumming sound, he danced and sang with a rhythm all his own. He danced in a backward motion. I was unable to make out his facial features because his head movements were so quick and sudden. I just saw a blur. It was very difficult to focus on his face. The song he sang was unrecognizable to me. Even the words he sang were strange. I was interested in knowing who this man was, but at the same time I was scared. It was very odd to see this man out there in the forest before me. I knew he was from another time long ago because of his clothes. As he danced, he raised his arms and soon began to motion towards the darkness. He motioned as if calling someone to join him in his dance. It was strange to see this faceless man dancing and motioning as he did. Then from the direction he was facing came another figure, a woman. She slowly entered the lit area and began to dance with the man. Unlike the man who sang throughout his dance, the woman remained silent. She danced in a forward direction, taking steps left then right, left then right. I was frozen with fear and amazement. I was as still as I could be. She was also dressed in old style clothes. She wore traditional leggings, and moccasins, and her hair was done up in the traditional pueblo woman manner. Over her back she wore a manta (a shawl worn over the shoulders and back). Although I was able to make out all the details of her outfit, her face was a blur also, and she was not someone I recognized. I kept quiet as they both danced in unison. I was mesmerized.

Suddenly, they made their way away from my camp and fire and moved towards the stream. It was at this point that I heard them both laughing. They soon disappeared by the stream and into the darkness of the night. During this "spiritual performance" I was unable to move my arms, legs or other

"Over her back she wore a manta."

part of my body. My eyes saw the vision and my ears heard the sounds. My focus was centered in simply observing and nothing more.

After they left me, I was alone with my thoughts. I knew what I had just witnessed was a spiritual sign. I was left mentally numb. I just sat there in a void.

Then again, I heard some sound coming from the north. I turned and saw what appeared to be flashlights coming my way through the forest. Great!, I thought, my buddies had seen my fire and located my whereabouts! There were three lights and they moved around in the darkness, coming closer and closer towards my direction. I was so relieved and happy that they had found me. After what I had just seen, they couldn't have come at a better time. As the lights came closer, they suddenly stopped about a hundred yards away. I threw more wood into the fire and waited. Expecting to see my friends faces any second, I sat back in my sleeping bag.

Out of the forest came three male figures, three men whom I did not recognize! As they got closer I saw that they had three horses with them. When they got to about fifty yards from me, I saw that they were Indians and were dressed in whiteman's clothes: Levi jackets, jeans, etc. Once they were close enough for me to hear their voices, I heard them speak in mumbling tones. I was unable to make out what they were saying. As soon as they spotted me, they stood still. I don't know why or how, but immediately I knew I was being visited by more spirits once again. As soon as this thought came over me, I closed my eyes and prayed. When I opened my eyes, the men were opposite the camp fire.

Then suddenly, in an instant, they had moved to another area of my camp, horses and all! Then in a blink of an eye, they were back where they were before, all seated and gazing in my direction.

Altogether, they extended their fingers towards me and pointed in a way that made me think I was something funny to them. They spoke, but all I could make out were mumbling sounds. At one point, one of the men bent forward to get a closer look at me. I looked at their horses and then at the fire which separated us. The man who had his eyes focused on me then let out a big laugh. I was scared. I must have passed out because when I came to, I found myself out of my sleeping bag, on the ground, several feet away from where I had been by the fire. I was on the cold ground shivering. The last thing I remembered was being in my sleeping bag, and now here I was freezing on the open ground several feet away. I got up and walked over to where the fire was. It was out, but there were still some hot glowing coals in the pit. I threw in more wood on top of the coals and soon I got a fire going again. I took my loaded pistol in one hand and a flashlight in the other and walked around the area where I had seen the three men. There was no sign that the ground or grass had been disturbed. I noticed that the sun was lighting up the sky before it made itself known above the mountains. As the light made the ground around me more visible, the only tracks I could find were the ones I had made coming into the meadow. There were no others. The grass was wet with dew and undisturbed.

I soon packed up my horse, cleaned camp, and rode up the ridge away from the meadow. I couldn't erase from my memory what had happened to me, just a few hours before. I was comforted by the morning sunlight that warmed my face and by the songs of the birds flying in and out of the trees.

Up in the distance I spotted my friends riding down the ridge. I heard them let out a yell and call out my name. I knew immediately these people were not spirits, but living human beings! As we met up with each other, my buddies had a shocked expression on each of their faces. "Hey Alfred, you look pretty pale," one guy said. "What happened to you?" I began to describe the night before to them. They freaked out! They were quiet throughout my story and when I was through, they began to tell me a story of their own.

They said that at about the same time that the spirits had appeared to me, they had all seen two Indian spirits! At first they heard the sound of footsteps running over the forest ground among the trees. Then a strange sense of someone watching them from the darkness overwhelmed them all. As they all sat quietly before their campfire, looking at each other, suddenly two Indian men dressed in old-style, warrior outfits came out of the forest, running at full speed right by them. Of course, they all knew something unusual and spiritual was taking place. The two warriors just raced by and disappeared into the forest from where they had come. After discussing among ourselves the possible reasons for what we had all experienced, we had no answers and were perplexed. I was apparently the most puzzled of all. I guess my friends saw this and decided that I needed to have a spiritual cleansing. My friends had me face north and in the afternoon sunlight I was prayed over in the Indian way, in order to remove the bad forces I might have been exposed to. We all headed back home and did not speak about what had happened any more.

That evening arriving at my house, I did mention my experience to my grandmother. She looked at me and listened to each word as if I was telling her something very important, something sacred. Then after I was through, she held my hands and informed me that she had some sad news for me. I was told that my other grandmother had died the same night I had had my vision. My grandmother also told me that what I had experienced was my other grandmother's way of showing me that she was all right and was now passing into the other world, the spirit world. Grandmother further informed me that the dancing man and woman headed in a southerly direction and disappeared because, "That's the spirits' way; they travel south. Where you were is where our Sacred Blue Lake is located. It's the spirits' way".

Grandmother then told me that the three men who showed themselves to me, after the two dancing spirits had left, were very different from the man and woman. "You know, those three spirits were very powerful. It was a good thing you did not speak to them. Keeping quiet was the best thing for you to do. Otherwise those spirits would have taken you away with them. You would have been left dead in the forest, your spirit would have been lifted away, and all we would have found would be your body. We would not have known what was the cause of your mysterious death. What saved you was the campfire that kept burning between where you were and where the spirits were. It was good that you asked the Creator for a blessing and for Mother Earth to protect you that night."

The story I have just told you is the truth. It is what I saw with my own eyes. There are people who do not believe in these things, but some do. I'm happy to know that my grandmother, who passed away, chose to let me know how she was and that she was headed to the spirit world. Because of the darkness that night, I could not recognize her. The dancing spirits were presented to me for a purpose; they were not bad or evil. But the other spirits, the three men... Well, I knew something was not right when I saw them.

You know, there are many other stories and incidents that have taken place in and around the pueblo. I have experienced some very strange things. There are such things as witches and evil doers, but I would rather not talk about them. To talk about them would only give them more strength and increase their power for doing bad.

Mountains above Taos Pueblo.

There are areas of power up here in the mountains, areas that feel negative to the soul. Indian people whom I've spoken to have told me that, as they travel through the forest, they can sometimes feel the presence of eyes gazing at them from between the trees. Some have even told me that they feel the presence of someone following them, something that moves from behind the trees, and hides among the shadows.

There are a lot of things that have happened to people around here. Most people prefer not to talk about them. Perhaps it's best not to. We'll leave it at that.

The End

Other Books
by
Red Rabbit Press

Adobe Angels-The Ghosts of Albuquerque
by
Antonio R. Garcez
Published 1994
ISBN 0-9634029-2-7

Recovery For Male Victims Of Child Sexual Abuse
by
Hank Estrada
Published 1994
ISBN 0-9634029-1-9

The above titles are available at all bookstores or
by writing directly to the publisher:

Red Rabbit Press
P.O. Box 6545
Santa Fe, NM 87502-6545